GROUP MEMBER

Proverbs: Uncommon Sense

Bible Study That Builds Christian Community

LifeWay | Small Groups

Proverbs: Uncommon Sense
Group Member Book

Fourth printing 2010

Published by Serendipity House Publishers
Nashville, Tennessee

ISBN 978-1-5749-4216-3
Item 001274642

Dewey Decimal Classification: 223.7
Subject Headings:
BIBLE.O.T. PROVERBS—STUDY \ CHRISTIAN LIFE

To purchase additional copies of this resource or other studies:
ORDER ONLINE at www.SerendipityHouse.com
WRITE Serendipity House, One LifeWay Plaza, Nashville, TN 37234-0175
FAX (615) 277-8181
PHONE (800) 458-2772

1-800-458-2772
www.SerendipityHouse.com

Printed in the United States of America

Barry E. Robert
Dec. 2011

Contents

Core Values

Community: The purpose of this curriculum is to build community within the body of believers around Jesus Christ.

Group Process: To build community, the curriculum must be designed to take a group through a step-by-step process of sharing your story with one another.

Interactive Bible Study: To share your "story," the approach to Scripture in the curriculum needs to be open-ended and right-brained—to "level the playing field" and encourage everyone to share.

Developmental Stages: To provide a healthy program in the life cycle of a group, the curriculum needs to offer courses on three levels of commitment:

(1) **Beginner Level**—low-level entry, high structure, to level the playing field;
(2) **Growth Level**—deeper Bible study, flexible structure, to encourage group accountability;
(3) **Discipleship Level**—in-depth Bible study, open structure, to move the group into high gear.

Target Audiences: To build community throughout the culture of the church, the curriculum needs to be flexible, adaptable, and transferable into the structure of the average church.

Mission: To expand the kingdom of God one person at a time by working together to fill the "empty chair." (We add an extra chair to each group session to remind us of our mission.)

Group Covenant

It is important that your group covenant together, agreeing to live out important group values. Once these values are agreed upon, your group will be on its way to experiencing Christian community. It's very important that your group discuss these values—preferably as you begin this study. The first session would be most appropriate. (Check the rules to which each member of your group agrees.)

- ▢ **Priority:** While you are in this course of study, you give the group meetings priority.
- ▢ **Participation:** Everyone is encouraged to participate and no one dominates.
- ▢ **Respect:** Everyone is given the right to his or her own opinion, and all questions are encouraged and respected.
- ▢ **Confidentiality:** Anything that is said in the meeting is never repeated outside the meeting.
- ▢ **Life Change:** We will regularly assess our own life-change goals and encourage one another in our pursuit of becoming more like Christ.
- ▢ **Empty Chair:** The group stays open to reaching new people at every meeting.
- ▢ **Care and Support:** Permission is given to call upon each other at any time, especially in times of crisis. The group will provide care for every member.
- ▢ **Accountability:** We agree to let the members of the group hold us accountable to the commitments we make in whatever loving ways we decide upon.
- ▢ **Mission:** We will do everything in our power to start a new group.
- ▢ **Ministry:** Members of the group will encourage one another to volunteer and serve in a ministry and to support missions by giving financially and/or personally serving.

notes

Session

1

A Priceless Pursuit

Proverbs 1:1-7

Prepare for the Session

1

	READINGS	REFLECTIVE QUESTIONS
Monday	Proverbs 1:1-6	How is your skill at living life right now? What areas of wisdom do you need to work on? How is justice and integrity related to wisdom?
Tuesday	Proverbs 1:7; 9:10-11	What unwise practices have ceased as you've grown to trust and love God more? How can wisdom add days to your life and *add to* your life?
Wednesday	Proverbs 2:1-5	What topic have you spent extended time studying? How valuable was the time you spent? How does a person listen closely to wisdom?
Thursday	Proverbs 3:5-6	Give examples of God's wisdom being counter to non-Christian thinking. Have you been hurt by following the world's wisdom instead of God's?
Friday	Proverbs 3:17-18	How does living life skillfully compare to the tree of life planted in the Garden of Eden? How can wisdom make a person happy? Why would anyone *not* want to follow God's wisdom?
Saturday	Proverbs 3:25-26	What have been some traps in your life? How have you allowed the Lord to be your confidence rather than depending on what you see and feel?
Sunday	Matthew 7:24-25	What does Matthew mean by the phrases "built his house on the rock" and "built his house on the sand"? Spiritually, how does a person learn the difference between "rock" and "sand"?

OUR GOALS FOR THIS SESSION ARE:

BIBLE STUDY

- To appreciate the different words used by Solomon for life-skill and how they can change our lives for the better
- To be motivated to study wisdom and consider it a priceless pursuit
- To understand that fearing God is the foundation of life-skill

LIFE CHANGE

- To write a journal account of incidents in which wisdom would have saved a lot of trouble and heartache
- To spend time in solitary prayer asking God if you have a healthy fear of Him
- To meditate on and memorize Proverbs 1:7

Icebreaker

10-15 minutes

GATHERING THE PEOPLE

Form horseshoe groups of 6-8.

Uncommon Sense. Depending on time, choose one or two questions, or answer all three. Go around the group on question 1 and let everyone share. Then go around again on questions 2 and 3.

1. When it comes to taking note of what is happening around me, my friends would say I'm most like the following zoo animal. Check the one that's the best fit.
   - ☐ Giraffe – the view I have is so different from everyone else's that I sometimes miss what others see.
   - ☐ Chimpanzee – Sometimes I'm so busy scratching my own itch that I don't notice anything except what's going on in my own cage.
   - ☐ Hawk – I can hover for hours looking for the one thing I want. When I find it, I swoop down and get it.
   - ☒ Turtle – I'm so busy; I just barely keep my own head above water.
   - ☐ Other: ______________________________

2. Describe a time when ignoring someone's advice caused you to do something embarrassing. What was the advice? What happened that embarrassed you because you didn't take that person's advice?

Driving late

3. Finish this sentence: The best advice ever given to me was . . .

Never quit!

Bible Study

30-45 minutes

The Scripture for this week:

LEARNING FROM THE BIBLE

PROVERBS 1:1-7

1 The proverbs of Solomon son of David, king of Israel:
2 For gaining wisdom and being instructed; for understanding
insightful sayings; 3 for receiving wise instruction [in] righteousness,
justice, and integrity; 4 or teaching shrewdness to the inexperienced,
knowledge and discretion to a young man— 5 a wise man will listen
and increase his learning, and a discerning man will obtain guidance— 6 for understanding a proverb or a parable, the words of the
wise, and their riddles.
7 The fear of the LORD is the beginning of knowledge; fools despise wisdom and instruction.

...about today's session

A WORD FROM THE LEADER

Write your answers here.

1. According to Solomon, what do his readers need to do?

Gain wisdom

2. What kinds of people does Solomon say need wisdom?

Wise people (All)

3. What is the attitude of fools?

despise wisdom & instruction (know it all)

Identifying with the Story

In horseshoe groups of 6-8, explore questions as time allows.

1. Tell a story about a lesson you learned the hard way that could have been avoided with a small amount of wisdom. Please tell your story in a paragraph, rather than book form.

Learned to keep mouth shut. Only give advice when asked. most just want to vent

2. Which one of the following areas is most likely to get you into trouble? Check one.

- ☐ Financial matters such as poor record keeping, savings, and planning
- ☐ The words that come out of my mouth
- ☐ Lack of desire to work hard at things I need to do
- ☐ Relationships with family
- ☐ A quick temper
- ☒ Resentment of authority or bad attitude toward criticism
- ☐ Failure to get advice or seek wisdom before acting
- ☐ Other: ____________________

3. What is the main obstacle to wisdom in your life? Check one.

☐ I don't read Proverbs or other biblical wisdom enough.
☐ I tend not to remember proverbs when I need them.
☐ I act too quickly without trying to think of a proverb or piece of advice.
☐ I have trouble applying a proverb to a real-life situation.
☐ Other:______________________________

today's session

What is God teaching you from this story?

1. What are the action verbs for learning in Proverbs 1:1-6?

2. What are the words used for wisdom in Proverbs 1:1-6?

3. Why are proverbs written as similes and catchy sayings?

4. What does Solomon mean by saying that fear of the Lord is the beginning of knowledge (verse 7)?

5. Is fear of the Lord an outdated concept?

Learning from the Story

In horseshoe groups of 6-8, explore these questions.

1. How do you feel about the concept of working consistently to learn wisdom?

- [ ] Sounds great, but I'm not good at follow-through.
- [ ] I am terrible at memorizing verses.
- [ ] I find Proverbs a hard book to read.
- [x] I would like to develop a plan for reading Proverbs daily.
- [ ] I would like to develop a plan for memorizing verses from Proverbs.
- [ ] I realize, in order to become all God wants me to become, I'm going to have to have a change of heart about the disciplines necessary to become wise. I'm going to begin asking God to transform my thinking.
- [ ] Other:____________________________________.

2. On a scale of 1 to 10, how would you grade your wisdom right now in the following areas and explain one of your answers to the group:

Family Life

1 2 3 4 5 6 7 8 9 10

"I feel totally inept in this area." — "I have in-depth understanding in this area."

Finances

1 2 3 4 5 6 7 8 9 10

"I feel totally inept in this area." — "I have in-depth understanding in this area."

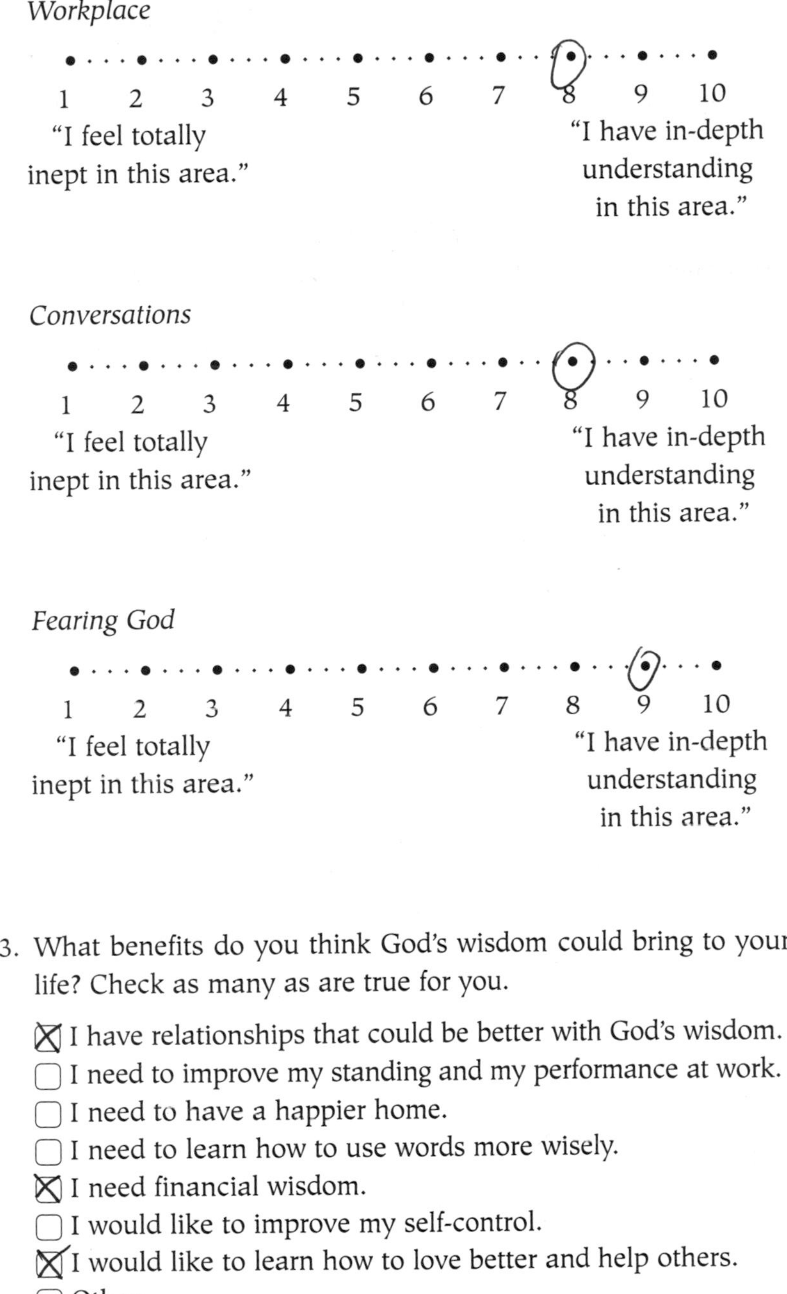

Workplace

1 2 3 4 5 6 7 8 9 10

"I feel totally inept in this area." — "I have in-depth understanding in this area."

Conversations

1 2 3 4 5 6 7 8 9 10

"I feel totally inept in this area." — "I have in-depth understanding in this area."

Fearing God

1 2 3 4 5 6 7 8 9 10

"I feel totally inept in this area." — "I have in-depth understanding in this area."

3. What benefits do you think God's wisdom could bring to your life? Check as many as are true for you.

- [x] I have relationships that could be better with God's wisdom.
- [ ] I need to improve my standing and my performance at work.
- [ ] I need to have a happier home.
- [ ] I need to learn how to use words more wisely.
- [x] I need financial wisdom.
- [ ] I would like to improve my self-control.
- [x] I would like to learn how to love better and help others.
- [ ] Other: ______________________________.

life change lessons

How can you apply this session to your life?

Write your answers here.

1. Think about this wonderful book of Proverbs that God has given us. What kinds of effort on your part will help you to use these proverbs to grow in wisdom and knowledge?

Read daily a proverb— and try to apply it!
–(memorize one)

2. Given your limited time and energy, what specific goals for improving your life could motivate you to work on wisdom?

Be useful in retirement (work)!

Caring Time

15-20 minutes

CARING TIME

Remain in horseshoe groups of 6-8.

This is the time to develop and express your caring for each other. Begin by asking group members to finish this sentence:

"What I would like to see happen in this group is ..."

Pray for these hopes as well as the concerns shared on the Prayer/Praise Report. Include prayer for the empty chair.

If you would like to pray silently, say "Amen" when you have finished your prayer, so that the next person will know when to start.

Reference Notes

BIBLE STUDY NOTES

Use these notes to gain further understanding of the text as you study on your own:

1

PROVERBS 1:2 *gaining wisdom.* The main theme in Proverbs is wisdom, the nature of it and how to obtain it. The proverbs are common-sense guidelines for living. They teach that wisdom begins with fearing the LORD (v. 7).

PROVERBS 1:7 *wise instruction.* Training in everyday actions, attitudes, and character that will lead to true success in life.

PROVERBS 1:7 *fear of the LORD.* The fear of the Lord involves acknowledging God's power and sovereignty, then offering our obedience in light of it. The fool disregards God's presence and power, acting as if personal satisfaction is all that matters.

PROVERBS 2:1-3 The writer repeatedly appeals to his son to live a life of wisdom.

PROVERBS 2:4 *seek ... treasure.* This is an apt comparison. To find treasure one must search, dig, and excavate. Finding wisdom requires similar activity.

PROVERBS 2:5 *then you will understand.* When we search for wisdom, we find God Himself, and our relationship with Him deepens.

PROVERBS 3:5 *with all your heart.* The Bible uses this phrase to express total commitment. The "Shema" in Deuteronomy 6:5 calls us to love God with all our hearts, minds, and souls. Jesus described this as the first and greatest commandment.

PROVERBS 3:6 *guide ... paths.* This implies more than guidance. It means God intentionally removes obstacles from our path.

notes

Session

2

Verbal Vices and Wise Words

Proverbs 12:14,18; 13:3; 18:2,8,13,21; 21:23; 29:5

Prepare for the Session

2

	READINGS	REFLECTIVE QUESTIONS
Monday	Proverbs 12:14; 13:3; 18:21	Is your mouth contributing as much to your well-being right now as your hands? Would you say that you are getting more sweet fruit or bitter fruit from your lips?
Tuesday	Proverbs 18:2,13	How hard is it for you to listen to other people? Why do you think listening is harder than expressing your own thoughts?
Wednesday	Proverbs 18:8	Why is gossip satisfying? What urges in us does it fulfill? Why do we gossip even when we know what we are saying could hurt or be untrue?
Thursday	Proverbs 12:18	How have you been hurt by the mean-spirited words of others? How have you hurt others with unkind words?
Friday	Proverbs 21:23	Is there a person or a group that brings out the worst in you when it comes to talking? Is there someone you know who frequently puts his foot in his mouth?
Saturday	Proverbs 29:5	What is the difference between encouragement and flattery?
Sunday	James 3:3-8	How does the tongue have so much influence over the way people perceive you? How hard is it to tame your tongue?

OUR GOALS FOR THIS SESSION ARE:

BIBLE STUDY

- To understand the consequences of rash words and angry responses
- To consider the motive behind verbal vices such as gossip and flattery
- To be motivated to use wise words to heal, repair, and help relationships

LIFE CHANGE

- To target someone for encouragement
- To ask a loved one how your words have hurt him or her in the past
- To meditate on and memorize Proverbs 12:18

Icebreaker

10-15 minutes

GATHERING THE PEOPLE

Form horseshoe groups of 6-8.

Think slow— later!

Tongue Taming. Depending on time, choose one or both questions to answer. Go around the group on question 1 and let everyone share. Then go around again on question 2.

1. If your words were hot sauce on chicken wings, which sauce best describes you when you're angry? Check one.

   - [ ] "No sauce on mine, please." – I never lash out at people when I'm angry.
   - [x] Mild sauce – I sometimes say things I shouldn't, but for the most part, I seldom hurt others with my remarks.
   - [ ] XXX sauce – I have to admit, sometimes my remarks are spiced with words not suitable for public consumption.
   - [ ] TNT sauce – I have a short fuse and have been known to lose control and verbally explode.
   - [ ] Other: ______________________________

2. If you could get a redo on one statement you've made in your lifetime, what would that statement be? Who did you say it to? How did making that statement affect your relationship with that person in both the short-term and long-term?

?

Probably when angry w/ children!
On refs at b-ball game!

2

Bible Study

30-45 minutes

The Scripture for this week:

LEARNING FROM THE BIBLE

PROVERBS 12:14,18; 13:3; 18:2,8,13,21; 21:23; 29:5

A man will be satisfied with good by the words of his mouth, and the work of a man's hands will reward him (Proverbs 12:14).

There is one who speaks rashly, like a piercing sword; but the tongue of the wise brings healing (Proverbs 12:18).

The one who guards his mouth protects his life; the one who opens his lips invites his own ruin (Proverbs 13:3).

A fool does not delight in understanding, but only wants to show off his opinions (Proverbs 18:2).

A gossip's words are like choice food that goes down to one's innermost being (Proverbs 18:8).

The one who gives an answer before he listens—this is foolishness and disgrace for him. (Proverbs 18:13)

Life and death are in the power of the tongue, and those who love it will eat its fruit (Proverbs 18:21).

The one who guards his mouth and tongue keeps himself out of trouble (Proverbs 21:23).

A man who flatters his neighbor spreads a net for his feet (Proverbs 29:5).

...about today's session

A WORD FROM THE LEADER

Write your answers here.

1. Why do our words matter so much in daily life?

2. According to this week's Scriptures, what are the benefits of wise words?

3. What sins and follies does Solomon describe in this week's Scriptures?

Identifying with the Story

In horseshoe groups of 6-8, explore questions as time allows.

1. When have you seriously damaged a relationship by something you said? How did the relationship turn out later, and what made it better or worse?

2. Which one of the following verbal vices irritates you the most? Check one.

- ☐ Spouting off ill-informed opinions as though an expert on the matter
- ☐ Flattering words that are completely insincere
- ☐ Talking negatively about you behind your back
- ☐ Talking negatively about someone else behind his or her back
- ☐ Insulting, denigrating language
- ☐ Answering you before listening to your real question or need
- ☐ Other:____

3. What positive example of using wisdom with words have you seen in someone else?

Ability to say "no" in a way that doesn't offend another.

today's session

2

What is God teaching you from this story?

1. What are some positive and negative consequences of words?

+ – help, encourage, uplift, positive self image
– – hurt, discourage, put down, neg. self-image
→ brings healing, has life, protects → ruin, death, disgrace

2. What are some examples of words that wound like a sword?

"dumb, idiot, worthless, stupid, ugly"

3. Why don't fools value listening as much as expressing their own opinion?

self-centered – don't want or need to learn
– know it all already

4. What exactly is gossip?

Speaking about someone – when not there
– negatively (usually)
– made to look bad
– harmfully

5. How is flattery a trap?

– it's a lie, and liars get caught
– communicates insincerity
– used to deceive

Learning from the Story

In horseshoe groups of 6-8, explore these questions.

1. From what you learned in these proverbs, which lesson will help you the most? Check one.

   - [x] Words have more effect than we think.
   - [ ] Insults and insulting humor can secretly devastate people.
   - [ ] Kind, truthful, and wise words can heal people.
   - [ ] Listening helps you learn and shows others you care.
   - [ ] Gossip is a cheap thrill that destroys friendships.
   - [ ] Flattery is insincere encouragement with a selfish motive.
   - [ ] Other: ______________________________.

2. Who is one person you would like to help by speaking wise words and encouragement to him/her this week?

   Mikayla & Mallory

3. What help do you need to improve your words? Check one.

   - [ ] God's help to think before speaking
   - [ ] Help from others to identify my own faults with words
   - [ ] Help from my spouse, closest family member, or closest friend to know how I have hurt them with words
   - [ ] God's help to value others more than myself
   - [x] God's help to know how to say what I mean and what I feel
   - [ ] Other: ______________________________

life change lessons

How can you apply this session to your life?

Write your answers here.

1. What motives lead us to use words wrongly?

   Self-centeredness!
   anger
   Impress

2. What motives lead us to use words to heal?

   Love for others.
   Compassion - "we care
   To please God!

Caring Time

15-20 minutes

CARING TIME

Remain in horseshoe groups of 6-8.

This is the time to develop and express your care for each other. Begin by asking group members to finish this sentence:

"What I like best about how we use words in this group is ..."

2

Pray for these encouragements to continue as well as the concerns of the Prayer/Praise Report. Include prayer for the empty chair.

If you would like to pray silently, say "Amen" when you have finished your prayer, so that the next person will know when to start.

Reference Notes

BIBLE STUDY NOTES

Use these notes to gain further understanding of the text as you study on your own:

PROVERBS 12:14 — ***words of his mouth.*** That is, literally, the words he speaks (25:11). The good things we do and say bring rewards.

PROVERBS 13:3 — ***guards his mouth.*** Words produce consequences. James reinforced the wisdom of taming the tongue (James 3:5-9).

PROVERBS 18:2 — A fool has no interest in learning, only in airing his own opinions.

PROVERBS 18:8 — ***choice food.*** This is an apt description of a "juicy" piece of gossip. Just as a delicacy is digested, gossip becomes a part of us and affects our attitudes.

PROVERBS 18:21 — ***Life and death.*** The tongue is the most powerful muscle in the body, but it also has incredible spiritual power in the lives of people. We can use use it to bring life or death to others and ourselves.

notes

Session

3

Relating Well, Relatively Speaking

Proverbs 14:1; 17:6; 18:22; 19:26; 23:15-16,26; 25:24; 27:8

Prepare for the Session

3

	READINGS	REFLECTIVE QUESTIONS
Monday	Proverbs 18:22	In what ways do you regard marriage as a blessing for yourself? For others? What statements do people often make contradicting this proverb?
Tuesday	Proverbs 23:15-16	What attitudes do you detect in this father as he speaks to his son? Do you regard children, both yours and other people's children, in this way?
Wednesday	Proverbs 27:8	What common societal problems is the writer referring to? According to this proverb, who is missing out or losing?
Thursday	Proverbs 14:1	What is contrasted in this proverb? In what ways are you building your home? How about ways you're tearing it down?
Friday	Proverbs 19:26	What is this verse saying about adults' relationships with their parents? How would you describe your relationship with your parents or your adult children's relationship with you?
Saturday	Proverbs 25:24	What common marital problem does this verse address? What alternatives are there to nagging?
Sunday	Proverbs 23:26	What method of rearing children is being advocated here? How does this compare to your own upbringing and/or your child rearing?

OUR GOALS FOR THIS SESSION ARE:

BIBLE STUDY

- To understand roles, relationships, and wisdom for families
- To be motivated to pursue or improve family relationships
- To begin to understand parenting and marriage according to God's timeless wisdom

LIFE CHANGE

- To talk with children about character issues and family wisdom
- To read a book that is biblical and helpful on a family issue of importance to us
- To memorize and meditate on a verse of your choice from this session

Icebreaker

10-15 minutes

GATHERING THE PEOPLE

Form horseshoe groups of 6-8.

Relatively Speaking. Depending on time, choose one or two questions, or answer all three. Go around the group on question 1 and let everyone share. If time allows, go around again on questions 2 and/or 3.

1. Which of the following movies reminds you most of relationships in your home when you were a child? Check one.

   ☐ *Parenthood* – we had a lot of problems, but we all loved each other deeply.

   ☐ *Star Wars* – every time I thought I had seen my last episode of conflict and battles, another episode occurred.

   ☐ *Saving Private Ryan* – if someone in the family was in a bad situation, we all did whatever it took to save him from himself or his difficult circumstances.

   ☐ *Castaway* – each of us lived his own life in his own world without connecting with anyone else.

   ☐ *King Kong* – dad was an intimidating giant and ruled the jungle we called home.

   ☒ Other: Peaceful ______________.

2. Finish the following statement: My parents' relationship with one another was most like a ...

   - ☐ Library – they seldom talked to one another.
   - ☐ Museum – mom and dad remembered past experiences without taking advantage of the possibilities to enjoy one another in the present.
   - ☐ Cruise ship – laughter and joking and fun were the norm.
   - ☐ Chemist's lab – they were always searching for the right formula for a happy marriage.
   - ☐ Church – prayer and Bible study were very much a part of their lives together.
   - ☒ Other: Average.

3

3. Which TV family would you have most liked to have grown up in? Why?

   - ☐ The Cleavers from *Leave It to Beaver*
   - ☒ The Ingalls from *Little House on the Prairie*
   - ☐ The Addams from *The Addams Family*
   - ☐ The Cartwrights from *Bonanza*
   - ☐ The Robinsons from *Lost in Space*
   - ☐ Other: ______________________

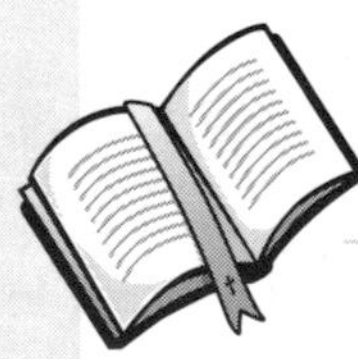

Bible Study

30-45 minutes

The Scripture for this week:

LEARNING FROM THE BIBLE

PROVERBS 14:1; 17:6; 18:22; 19:26; 23:15-16,26; 25:24; 27:8

Every wise woman builds her house, but a foolish one tears it down with her own hands (Proverbs 14:1).

Grandchildren are the crown of the elderly, and the pride of sons is their fathers (Proverbs 17:6).

A man who finds a wife finds a good thing and obtains favor from the LORD (Proverbs 18:22).

The one who assaults his father and evicts his mother is a disgraceful and shameful son (Proverbs 19:26).

BIBLE STUDY (cont'd)

My son, if your heart is wise, my heart will indeed rejoice. My innermost being will cheer when your lips say what is right (Proverbs 23:15-16).

My son, give me your heart, and let your eyes observe my ways (Proverbs 23:26).

Better to live on the corner of a roof than in a house shared with a nagging wife (Proverbs 25:24).

A man wandering from his home is like a bird wandering from its nest (Proverbs 27:8).

...about today's session

A WORD FROM THE LEADER

Write your answers here.

1. Who created the family? How was it created?

God

God said

2. What does Paul remind us of concerning the command to honor parents?

Eph 6:1; Col 3:20 - "obey"

Rom 1:30 - disobedient to parents

II Cor 12:14 - parents save for children

* Eph 6:2 1st commandment w/ promise! "live long in the land God is giving you."

3. What are the most important traits of a healthy family?

Love

Servanthood

Communication

Patience

(Respect)

Identifying with the Story

In horseshoe groups of 6-8, explore questions as time allows.

1. Relate a favorite family memory.

Family picnics - Alpine beach

- Cowan's Gap

- Caledonia

2. Which areas about family are you most interested in discussing? Check one.

- ☐ How to avoid quarreling and nagging
- ☐ How to become a mentor, not just a slave-master, for my children
- ☐ How to develop a relationship between my kids and my parents
- ☐ How to be a good father or mother
- ☐ How to think about the value of marriage
- ☐ How to think of my parents now that I am an adult
- ☒ How to be a good grandparent
- ☐ Other: ______________________

3

3. What prevents you from being the best family member you can be? Check one.

- ☐ I have trouble balancing career and family.
- ☐ I simply don't know scriptural principles for family life.
- ☐ I have better theories than actual practice in my family life.
- ☐ I have family members who are difficult.
- ☒ Other: time restraints

today's session

What is God teaching you from this story?

1. In what way does the Bible view a spouse as a blessing?

"helper suitable for him" — "find favor with Lord"

2. How would you define nagging? What is the difference between nagging and quarreling?

constant barrage of suggestions, demands, or interruptions
quarreling – anger involved
fighting, antagonistic

3. Who ends up hurt the most when a spouse abandons a family?

the children

TODAY'S SESSION (cont'd)

4. What are some myths about the role of a homemaker?

2nd class citizen
not worth much!!
(not very rewarding!)

5. According to Solomon, what is the best method of rearing children?

By example & teaching
Prov. 23:26

Learning from the Story

In horseshoe groups of 6-8, explore these questions.

1. How do you feel about your upbringing? Check one.
   - ☐ Mom and Dad did not know the Bible, but they did pretty well.
   - ☐ Mom and Dad made mistakes that still hurt.
   - ☐ My parents cared but spent little time with me.
   - ☐ I was hurt by one of my parents abandoning our family.
   - ☐ I missed out on the joy of grandparents.
   - ☒ While no family is perfect, my parents spent time with me and cared for me.
   - ☐ Other:______________________________________.

2. In what ways are you imitating your parents or purposefully trying to avoid their mistakes?

Talking more w/ Flo.

3. In which area of Solomon's wisdom do you have the most problem right now? Check one.

- ☐ Viewing marriage as a blessing
- ☐ Learning better ways to communicate than quarreling and nagging
- ☐ Appreciating my parents
- ☒ Spending time with my grandchildren will change
- ☐ Valuing my role in my family
- ☐ Mentoring my children
- ☐ Other: ___________________________

3

life change lessons

How can you apply this session to your life?

Write your answers here.

1. What is the first step to a better family life?

Have a plan.

2. What habits and attitudes need to be unlearned to make your family life better?

Non-communication

Caring Time

15-20 minutes

CARING TIME

Remain in horseshoe groups of 6-8.

This is the time to develop and express your care for each other. Begin by having group members respond to this question:

"Where do you struggle most in your family life, and how can we pray for you?"

Pray for these concerns, as well as the concerns shared on the Prayer/Praise Report. Include prayer for the empty chair.

If you would like to pray silently, say "Amen" when you have finished your prayer, so that the next person will know when to start.

Reference Notes

BIBLE STUDY NOTES

Use these notes to gain further understanding of the text as you study on your own:

PROVERBS 14:1

builds her house. The focus here is on "house," which refers to a home. Providing a solid foundation for her family is one of a wise woman's great achievements.

PROVERBS 18:22

finds a good thing. A good wife is a treasure and gift from God. We need to appreciate the wife or husband that God has put into our life.

PROVERBS 19:26

assaults. In this culture the care of elderly parents was the responsibility of sons and daughters.

PROVERBS 23:16

innermost being. This literally means "kidneys" and refers to who we really are at the core of our being; the real, deepest person that we are.

PROVERBS 27:8

man wandering. When a man leaves home, he leaves not only responsibility but also protection behind.

notes

3

notes

Session

4

Ticked Off!

Proverbs 10:12; 15:1; 16:32; 17:1,9,14; 19:11

Prepare for the Session

	READINGS	REFLECTIVE QUESTIONS
Monday	Proverbs 10:12; 17:9	What offenses bother you often? How good are you at covering offenses with love? When problems occur, what does it take for you to forgive?
Tuesday	Proverbs 15:1	What do you do when tempted to return insult for insult? How did Jesus respond to insults?
Wednesday	Proverbs 16:32	Think about the patient people you admire. What have they done to model patience for you? How patient has God been with you lately?
Thursday	Proverbs 17:1	Have you experienced a strife-filled house? Does your faith in Jesus help you reduce strife in your home? If not, why? What kind of model are you being for your children?
Friday	Proverbs 17:14	Ever realized in the middle of an argument that you could have prevented it? How is quarreling hurting your life? Recall the last two issues you argued about. How important were they really?
Saturday	Proverbs 19:11	What or who helps you have patience and self-control? How can God help you grow more here?
Sunday	James 1:19-20	What would happen if you consistently followed James' advice (to be slow to speak and quick to hear) in your home or at work? What results would this bring?

OUR GOALS FOR THIS SESSION ARE:

BIBLE STUDY

- To recognize the destructive power of anger
- To learn practical tools for reducing conflict and controlling temper
- To learn the wisdom of patience and long-suffering

LIFE CHANGE

- To make amends with someone with whom you frequently quarrel
- To list offenses that usually anger you but which you can choose to overlook
- To meditate on and memorize Proverbs 19:11

Icebreaker

10-15 minutes

GATHERING THE PEOPLE

Form horseshoe groups of 6-8.

Flaring Up. Depending on time, choose one or two questions, or answer all three. Go around the group on question 1 and let everyone share. If time allows, go around again on questions 2, 3, and/or 4.

1. When you were in high school, what did your parents expect of you that caused your blood to boil?

2. Finish the following statement: "The last time I got really frustrated was when ..." Check one and share it with you group.

   - ☐ Traffic wasn't moving at my pace
   - ☐ My spouse knew we were supposed to leave to go someplace but wasn't ready on time
   - ☐ My children didn't do as they were told
   - ☐ My co-workers did their job poorly
   - ☐ A friend gave me a tongue lashing
   - ☐ Other: ______________________

3. Refer to your answer to question two. What did you do or say because you were upset?

grumble
tongue lashing

4. Who is the most patient person you've ever known? What word or phrase describes how you feel about that person?

Rachel – 3 little ones

Bible Study

30-45 minutes

The Scripture for this week:

LEARNING FROM THE BIBLE

PROVERBS 10:12; 15:1; 16:32; 17:1,9,14; 19:11

Hatred stirs up conflicts, but love covers all offenses (Proverbs 10:12).

A gentle answer turns away anger, but a harsh word stirs up wrath (Proverbs 15:1).

Patience is better than power, and controlling one's temper, than capturing a city (Proverbs 16:32).

Better a dry crust with peace than a house full of feasting with strife (Proverbs 17:1).

Whoever conceals an offense promotes love, but whoever gossips about it separates friends (Proverbs 17:9).

To start a conflict is to release a flood; stop the dispute before it breaks out (Proverbs 17:14).

A person's insight gives him patience, and his virtue is to overlook an offense (Proverbs 19:11).

...about today's session

A WORD FROM THE LEADER

Write your answers here.

1. What evidence is there that we actually can control our anger?

2. What are the different kinds of anger?

3. What is the relationship between anger and strife?

Identifying with the Story

In horseshoe groups of 6-8, explore questions as time allows.

1. What is the most embarrassing thing you have done in public because of anger?

2. Which of the following anger reactions have you been guilty of? Check all that apply.

- [ ] Shunning a friend or loved one for more than a week
- [ ] Yelling in public and making a scene
- [ ] Starting a fight while we were supposed to be having fun on vacation
- [ ] Insulting or calling a friend or loved one an inappropriate name
- [ ] Treating a sales clerk or waiter rudely
- [x] Giving someone the silent treatment
- [ ] Nearly causing a traffic accident
- [ ] Other:______________________________

3. What makes you the angriest? Check one.
   - [ ] When someone insults my intelligence
   - [ ] When someone cuts in front of me
   - [ ] When someone makes me wait
   - [ ] When someone makes a rude gesture or insulting comment
   - [ ] When someone doesn't listen to what I tell them to do
   - [x] Other: When bad guys prosper!

today's session

What is God teaching you from this story?

4

1. How does love regard the other person?

   Looks out for their best! — better than ourselves

2. What does love do with offenses (Prov. 10:12; 17:9)?

   Covers up or conceals.

3. What does our sinful nature prompt us to do in response to insults and anger?

   Hit back! Retaliate!

4. What proves that we can control our temper?

   Some people do it!

5. When is the best time to stop a fight?

   Before it starts!

Learning from the Story

In horseshoe groups of 6-8, explore these questions.

1. What situation commonly makes it hard for you to keep your temper?

   ☐ When a family member speaks unkindly to me
   ☒ When I'm under pressure and someone makes me wait
   ☐ When people are rude in traffic
   ☐ When sales clerks or food servers are slow or incompetent
   ☐ When people at work act foolishly or rudely
   ☐ Other:______________________________

2. On a scale of 1-10, how would you evaluate your daily battle with anger and conflict right now?

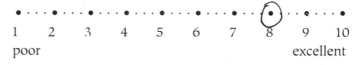

   1 2 3 4 5 6 7 (8) 9 10
   poor — excellent

3. If you were to describe your anger, which metaphor would fit best? Check one.

   ☐ A keg of gunpowder
   ☐ A firecracker
   ☐ A slow-burning fire
   ☐ A gentle breeze
   ☒ Other: ________________

life change lessons

How can you apply this session to your life?

Write your answers here.

1. What wrong beliefs do you need to address in order to begin growing out of any areas of anger or temper?

   "I can do everything" → time pressure → frustration. – "Margin"

2. Which key practice or belief do you need to adopt in order to replace quarreling with more constructive communication?

   "I need to do everything."

Caring Time

15-20 minutes

CARING TIME

Remain in horseshoe groups of 6-8.

This is the time to develop and express your care for each other. Begin by asking group members to respond to this question:

"What personal struggle do you need encouragement for this week?"

Pray for these struggles, as well as the concerns identified in the Prayer/Praise Report. Include prayer for the empty chair.

If you would like to pray silently, say "Amen" when you have finished your prayer, so that the next person will know when to start.

4

Reference Notes

BIBLE STUDY NOTES

Use these notes to gain further understanding of the text as you study on your own:

PROVERBS 15:1

Much like James, Proverbs makes the point that the way we use speech tells a lot about what kind of people we are (James 3:5-8). Whether we use gentle or harsh words, our conversation reflects our character.

PROVERBS 17:1

feasting. This refers to feasting provided for by a family's peace offering. See Levitcus 7:12-17.

PROVERBS 17:9

conceals. To conceal a sin is to literally overwhelm it with forgiveness and love.

notes

Session

5

Me, Me, and Oh Yeah – Me

Proverbs 11:2; 12:9; 16:18-19; 18:12; 22:4; 25:6-7; 27:1-2,21

Prepare for the Session

	READINGS	REFLECTIVE QUESTIONS
Monday	Proverbs 11:2; 16:18	Think about a time when your own pride caused you a problem. What happened? What is pride, and where does it come from?
Tuesday	Proverbs 18:12; 25:6-7	Do you like to honor people who are humble, or do you consider them weak and stupid? Why do people oftentimes love a humble person?
Wednesday	Proverbs 27:1	Why does boasting about the future indicate pride? What is the truth about your future plans, even your plans for today?
Thursday	Proverbs 27:2, 21	Is it wrong to receive praise? Do you rely on praise from others to feel good about yourself? Do you give praise to others?
Friday	Proverbs 12:9; 16:19	How often do you shade the truth to make yourself look better to others? Are you content to be with people who are not popular or well-to-do?
Saturday	Proverbs 22:4; James 4:6	Think about your prayer times. Do you approach God as if He's obligated to help you? Why does God reward humility?
Sunday	Philippians 2:8	In what ways was humbling for Jesus to become a man and die on the cross. What motivated His humility? How can you learn from this?

OUR GOALS FOR THIS SESSION ARE:

BIBLE STUDY

- To know what humility is and what it looks like when put into practice
- To see humility as the heart of God's calling for our lives
- To rehearse truths that will enable us to put humility into practice

LIFE CHANGE

- To practice focusing on others with an occasion when we won't talk about ourselves
- To improve our habit of humility by listing some activities we can do for others, then following through with those activities
- To meditate on and memorize Proverbs 18:12

Icebreaker

10-15 minutes

GATHERING THE PEOPLE

Form horseshoe groups of 6-8.

Who Am I? Depending on time, choose one or two questions, or answer all three. Be sure you go around the group on question 1 and let everyone share. Then go around again on questions 2 and 3.

1. What is the most hilarious practical joke you ever played on someone?

Bryan Reid – b-day party
– 40th
– Viagra hat – "Mark Martin"
– truck door

Dale @ Harvey Cedars
(Bob)

2. Which description best depicts your ego when you were sixteen years old?

- ☐ Non-existent – My self-image was so low there was no room for an ego.
- ☐ Unknown – I believed I was really something but seldom tried to prove it.
- ☒ Overshadowed – The friends I hung out with were so over the top on the ego chart that I found out I had an ego only later in life.
- ☐ Off the charts – I mistakenly believed I was the best at anything I tried to do.
- ☐ Other: ______________________________.

3. Of all the people you've come in contact with, who deserves an apology from you the most? Why?

Bible Study

30-45 minutes

The Scripture for this week:

LEARNING FROM THE BIBLE

PROVERBS 11:2; 12:9; 16:18-19; 18:12; 22:4; 25:6-7; 27:1-2,21

When pride comes, disgrace follows, but with humility comes wisdom (Proverbs 11:2).

Better to be dishonored, yet have a servant, than to act important but have no food (Proverbs 12:9).

Pride comes before destruction, and an arrogant spirit before a fall (Proverbs 16:18).

Better to be lowly of spirit with the humble than to divide plunder with the proud (Proverbs 16:19).

Before his downfall a man's heart is proud, but before honor comes humility (Proverbs 18:12).

The result of humility is fear of the LORD, along with wealth, honor, and life (Proverbs 22:4).

Don't brag about yourself before the king, and don't stand in the place of the great; for it is better for him to say to you, "Come up here!" than to demote you in plain view of a noble (Proverbs 25:6-7).

Don't boast about tomorrow, for you don't know what a day might bring (Proverbs 27:1). Let another praise you, and not your own mouth—a stranger, and not your own lips (Proverbs 27:2).

Silver is tested in a crucible, gold in a smelter, and a man, by the praise he receives (Proverbs 27:21).

...about today's session

A WORD FROM THE LEADER

Write your answers here.

1. What are some false ideas about humility?

2. What is humility really?

3. What are some benefits of humility for us? For others in our lives?

Identifying with the Story

In horseshoe groups of 6-8, explore questions as time allows.

1. Tell a story about seeing a humble person receive recognition or reward. Share how you felt about it.

2. Which prideful behavior makes you angriest? Check one.

☐ A person who boasts about his importance, skill, or future chance of success
☐ A person who always presumes to be first in line
☐ A person of higher status who assumes a place of privilege
☐ A person of lower status who talks big and assumes a greater place
☐ People who talk about themselves all the time
☐ A person who always expects you to serve him
☐ Other: ____________________

3. What aspect of humility is hardest for you? Check one.

   - [ ] To listen to others and care more about what they say than what I want to say
   - [ ] To perform physical tasks for loved ones instead of assuming they'll do them for me
   - [ ] To give time to other people in spite of my busy schedule
   - [ ] To genuinely regard strangers and acquaintances as more important than myself
   - [ ] To genuinely regard loved ones as more important than myself
   - [ ] Other:________________________________

today's session

What is God teaching you from this story?

1. What are some other words for pride?

2. What is presumption?

3. Why does pride lead to a downfall?

4. Why is boasting about the future a sin?

5. How is praise from others a test of character?

5

Learning from the Story

In horseshoe groups of 6-8, explore these questions.

1. How do you feel about developing humility? Check one.

   ☐ Too late! I'm already humble.
   ☐ Impossible. I've thought me-first for so long I doubt I can change.
   ☐ It will be hard, but it will be worth the attitude adjustment.
   ☒ I've got to because I want my life to count for good and not be self-seeking.
   ☐ I've thought about this a lot, but this subject is one I always need to relearn.
   ☐ Other:______________________________________.

2. How would you interpret the following statement: "Take pride in yourself"?

3. What benefits do you think come from increased humility? Check all that apply.

   ☒ I would enjoy other people more, such as my family and friends.
   ☐ I might make more friends and have deeper relationships.
   ☐ I might have a smoother life with God's blessing and the goodwill of others.
   ☒ I might be able to help some people I care about if I thought about myself less.
   ☐ I might have a more balanced life.
   ☐ Other: ______________________________________.

life change lessons

How can you apply this session to your life?

Write your answers here.

1. How can the Holy Spirit help you to overcome conceit and arrogance?

2. What are some practical steps to increasing humility?

Caring Time

15-20 minutes

CARING TIME

Remain in horseshoe groups of 6-8.

This is the time to develop and express your care for each other. Begin by asking group members to answer these questions:

"Where do you see the most urgent need for humility in your life? How can this group pray for you?"

Pray for these needs, as well as the concerns captured on the Prayer/Praise Report. Include prayer for the empty chair.

If you would like to pray silently, say "Amen" when you have finished your prayer, so that the next person will know when to start.

BIBLE STUDY NOTES

Reference Notes

Use these notes to gain further understanding of the text as you study on your own:

PROVERBS 11:2 ***humility.*** This refers to putting both God and others before yourself. See also Micah 6:8.

PROVERBS 12:9 ***have a servant.*** It's better to be of humble circumstances working for yourself than acting big yet having nothing to eat.

PROVERBS 25:6 ***place of the great.*** We should never "toot our own horn" or honor ourselves. The circumstance here is a feast, in shich we are instructed never to take the place of honor, assuming our own greatness.

PROVERBS 27:21 ***crucible.*** Our response to praise is a test of of our true charcater. Silver and gold are purified with heat. Our character is also tested in the heat of life.

Session

6

Friends and Enemies

Proverbs 12:25; 14:21,31; 17:17; 18:24; 20:6; 21:21; 22:9; 24:17-18; 25:21-22; 28:27

Prepare for the Session

	READINGS	REFLECTIVE QUESTIONS
Monday	Proverbs 14:21; 21:21	What is the link between kindness and happi ness? Why is a kind person honored? Do you show kindness to both friends and strangers?
Tuesday	Proverbs 12:25	What kind word recently encouraged you? Do you use your words to uplift or to promote yourself at the expense of others? Why do you do that?
Wednesday	Proverbs 20:6	How big is the difference between your walk of friendship and your talk? Do you often tell people you'll do something and not follow through?
Thursday	Proverbs 14:31; 22:9; 28:27	What is especially hard about helping a poor person? How are people who help the poor blessed?
Friday	Proverbs 17:17; 18:24	Who are your friends, and whose friendship is most important to you? Why? How loyal are you to your friends?
Saturday	Proverbs 24:17-18; 25:21-22	Do you have any personal enemies? Why should we love our enemies? Does God love His enemies? Were you ever God's enemy?
Sunday	John 13:34-35	Who is Jesus calling you to love in these verses? How are you fulfilling this command?

OUR GOALS FOR THIS SESSION ARE:

BIBLE STUDY

- To better understand the benefits and importance of kindness
- To begin to see kindness and a loving spirit as the center of a successful, Christ-like life
- To be prepared before we encounter people to treat them with kindness

LIFE CHANGE

- To realize who your true friends are and how you can be a better friend
- To volunteer as a way to develop love for people in need
- To memorize and meditate on Proverbs 21:21

Icebreaker

10-15 minutes

GATHERING THE PEOPLE

Form horseshoe groups of 6-8.

What Are Friends For?. Depending on time, choose one or two questions, or answer all three. Go around the group on question 1 and let everyone share. Then go around again on questions 2 and 3.

1. Which of the following sports best describes the relationship you had with your best friends in high school? Check one.

   - [x] Tennis – We saw life as an individual sport; there was little or no reason to help each other out.
   - [ ] Synchronized Swimming – We sometimes didn't notice that someone needed us until he was already drowning in a difficult situation.
   - [ ] Basketball – We assisted each other any time there was a need.
   - [ ] Boxing – We fought with each other much of the time.
   - [ ] Eco Challenge – I wouldn't have made it without them.
   - [ ] Other: ______________________________

2. Imagine that you have been forced to choose three friends outside your immediate family to live the rest of your life with on another planet. You will never be with anyone but those three people for the rest of your life. Whom will you choose? What one characteristic do all three of these people exhibit?

3. Describe a conflict between you and a friend where loyalty was the only thing that saved the friendship.

Bible Study

30-45 minutes **6**

The Scripture for this week:

LEARNING FROM THE BIBLE

PROVERBS 12:25; 14:21,31; 17:17; 18:24; 20:6; 21:21; 22:9; 24:17-18; 25:21-22; 28:27

Anxiety in a man's heart weighs it down, but a good word cheers it up (Proverbs 12:25).

The one who despises his neighbor sins, but whoever shows kindness to the poor will be happy (Proverbs 14:21).

The one who oppresses the poor insults their Maker, but one who is kind to the needy honors Him (Proverbs 14:31).

A friend loves at all times, and a brother is born for a difficult time (Proverbs 17:17).

A man with many friends may be harmed, but there is a friend who stays closer than a brother (Proverbs 18:24).

Many a man proclaims his own loyalty, but who can find a trustworthy man? (Proverbs 20:6).

The one who pursues righteousness and faithful love will find life, righteousness, and honor (Proverbs 21:21).

BIBLE STUDY (cont'd)

A generous person will be blessed, for he shares his food with the poor (Proverbs 22:9).

Don't gloat when your enemy falls, and don't let your heart rejoice when he stumbles, or the LORD will see, be displeased, and turn His wrath away from him (Proverbs 24:17-18).

If your enemy is hungry, give him food to eat, and if he is thirsty, give him water to drink; for you will heap coals on his head, and the LORD will reward you (Proverbs 25:21-22).

The one who gives to the poor will not be in need, but one who turns his eyes away will receive many curses (Proverbs 28:27).

...about today's session

A WORD FROM THE LEADER

Write your answers here.

1. What are some examples of me-centered thinking that prevent me from showing kindness?

Wrapped up in work.
In a hurry!

2. What is the relationship between humility and love?

Hard to love if it's all about you!

3. What are some earthly and heavenly benefits to showing love and kindness?

Earthly – peace;
Heavenly – blessing of God

Identifying with the Story

In horseshoe groups of 6-8, explore questions as time allows.

1. Tell a story about an unusual kindness someone has shown to you or to someone else.

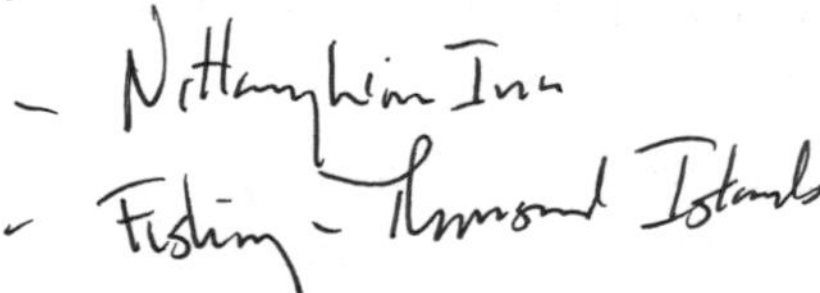

2. Which acts of kindness are hardest for you? Check all that apply.

- [ ] Letting others go first in a grocery store line
- [x] Letting others in front of me in a traffic situation
- [ ] Visiting a person who is ill or bereaved
- [x] Visiting someone in prison
- [ ] Talking to someone who is distraught or depressed
- [ ] Giving money or time to someone who needs help
- [ ] Saying something encouraging to someone
- [ ] Other:________________________

3. Summarize the most moving love story you've read, heard, seen, or experienced.

Man & wife w/ Alzheimer's

today's session

What is God teaching you from this story?

1. What kind of love gets the most attention?

- romantic (cc. Hollywood!)

2. What other kinds of love are there?

brotherly
agape

3. Why is having too many friends harmful?

How can you do it!

4. Why is it especially praiseworthy to love strangers, enemies, and the needy? Easy to love those who love you!

5. How does loving our enemies bring judgment on them?

- God's part.
- May convict or embarass them.

6

Learning from the Story

In horseshoe groups of 6-8, explore these questions.

1. What issues are involved for you in improving your habits of love and kindness? Check all that apply.

- [x] These habits are important to me, but I need to keep reminding myself.
- [x] I need to develop more deep friendships.
- [x] Loving enemies is difficult for me.
- [ ] I have to develop love for strangers and needy people.
- [ ] I need to be more encouraging and less critical to others.
- [ ] I try to be friends with too many people. I need to have deeper friendships with a few people with whom I can be honest.

2. Finish this sentence: "I would be more loving if ..."

I took the time! ~ "Self-absorbed"

3. What aspects of friendship do you need to work on the most? Check one.

- [x] I need to give my friends more of my time.
- [ ] I need to learn who my friends really are.
- [ ] I need to be ready for my friends when they need me.
- [ ] I need to reduce the number of people with whom I'm trying to be friends.
- [ ] Other: ______________________________.

life change lessons

How can you apply this session to your life?

Write your answers here.

1. Is emotional affection necessary to love people? Explain.

No! - Agape love is objective - "acts"

2. What are some practical steps to growing in love?

Look for ways!
Just do it!

Caring Time

15-20 minutes

CARING TIME

Remain in horseshoe groups of 6-8.

This is the time to develop and express your care for each other. Begin by asking group members to answer this question:

"How can we love each other more in this group?"

Pray for these needs as well as the concerns on listed on the Prayer/Praise Report. Include prayer for the empty chair.

If you would like to pray silently, say "Amen" when you have finished your prayer, so that the next person will know when to start.

Reference Notes

BIBLE STUDY NOTES

Use these notes to gain further understanding of the text as you study on your own:

6

PROVERBS 14:21 ***despises.*** Holds in contempt, belittles, ridicules. God held the whole nation responsible for their poor neighbors.

PROVERBS 14:31 God is a protector of the poor (22:22-23). Our actions toward the poor reflect our attitude toward God.

PROVERBS 24:17-18 ***gloat.*** An attitude of superiority. God detests this attitude—even when we gloat over adversaries.

PROVERBS 25:21 ***If your enemy.*** Jesus taught this in Luke 6:27-31.

PROVERBS 25:22 ***heap coals.*** When a fire went out, the homeowner would often borrow burning coals from a neighbor to start the fire again. In Egyptian culture carrying burning coals on one's head was a ritual of repentance. (See also Romans 12:20.)

notes

Session

7

Lie, Cheat and Steal

Proverbs 11:20; 12:22; 13:6; 14:25; 19:1,28; 20:17; 21:6; 28:6

Prepare for the Session

	READINGS	REFLECTIVE QUESTIONS
Monday	Proverbs 19:1; 28:6	Have you ever saved money or received money dishonestly? What reaction did the Holy Spirit have in your spirit to dishonesty?
Tuesday	Psalm 15:1-5	Which actions listed in this psalm are suprising to you? With a list like this, how many people do can live on God's "holy mountain"? How do you feel knowing that Jesus made a way for you?
Wednesday	Proverbs 20:17; 21:6	Why do you think the writer compares a fraudulent fortune to a "pursuit of death"? Would you be tempted to get rich by lying if you knew a way? Do you think you might follow through?
Thursday	Proverbs 11:20; 12:22	Would you rather be a delight to the Lord or get away with a lie for gain? Talk to God honestly about your level of sincerity with others.
Friday	Proverbs 13:6	How would you define *integrity*? When people believe you to be a person of integrity, what are the results?
Saturday	Proverbs 14:25; 19:28	Other than in court, what ways can you be a false witness? Why does God hate this?
Sunday	Psalm 25:1-3	Would you be able to pray like David here? Is it naïve to believe in God's protection for honesty?

OUR GOALS FOR THIS SESSION ARE:

BIBLE STUDY

- To understand the severity of dishonesty in God's eyes
- To develop faith in God's blessing for living honestly
- To grow in a desire to live at peace with God through honesty

LIFE CHANGE

- To list the ways that lying and cheating are affecting or have affected your life
- To confess a sin of dishonesty to a trusted friend
- To meditate on Proverbs 11:20 and memorize it

Icebreaker

10-15 minutes

GATHERING THE PEOPLE

Form horseshoe groups of 6-8.

Shading the Truth. Depending on time, choose one or two questions, or answer all three. Go around the group on question 1 and let everyone share. Then go around again on questions 2 and/or 3 if time allows.

1. The most dishonest thing I remember doing before age 10 is ...

- ☐ cheating on a test
- ☐ copying someone else's homework
- ☒ taking change or candy from my parents when they weren't looking
- ☐ hiding under the blanket with a flashlight reading or playing with toys after bedtime
- ☐ doing something to a younger sibling and telling him he'd be in big trouble if he told on me
- ☐ Other: ____________________

2. When someone lies to me, my instinctive reaction is to . . .

☐ Hurt him	☒ Never trust him again
☐ Forgive him	☐ Break off my relationship with him
☐ Confront him	☐ Other: ______________

3. What's the most devastating lie you were ever told? How did that affect your relationship with the person that lied to you?

Bible Study

30-45 minutes

The Scripture for this week:

LEARNING FROM THE BIBLE

PROVERBS 11:20; 12:22; 13:6; 14:25; 19:1,28; 20:17; 21:6; 28:6

Those with twisted minds are detestable to the LORD, but those with blameless conduct are His delight (Proverbs 11:20).

Lying lips are detestable to the LORD, but faithful people are His delight (Proverbs 12:22).

Righteousness guards people of integrity, but wickedness undermines the sinner (Proverbs 13:6).

A truthful witness rescues lives, but one who utters lies is deceitful (Proverbs 14:25).

Better a poor man who walks in integrity than someone who has deceitful lips and is a fool (Proverbs 19:1).

A worthless witness mocks justice, and a wicked mouth swallows iniquity (Proverbs 19:28).

Food gained by fraud is sweet to a man, but afterwards his mouth is full of gravel (Proverbs 20:17).

Making a fortune through a lying tongue is a vanishing mist, a pursuit of death (Proverbs 21:6).

Better a poor man who lives with integrity than a rich man who distorts right and wrong (Proverbs 28:6).

...about today's session

A WORD FROM THE LEADER

Write your answers here.

1. What is the difference between our dishonesty and someone else's?

   We excuse ours!

2. What is Jesus teaching when He says, "Let your word 'yes' be 'yes' " (Matthew 5:37)?

   Say what you mean!

3. What is a common, dishonest practice of Jesus-followers regarding promises to pray?

   Forget to do it!

Identifying with the Story

In horseshoe groups of 6-8, explore questions as time allows.

1. Tell a story about someone being unusually honest.

2. What kinds of lies bother you the most? Check all that apply.

   - [ ] Phony religious talk or promises to pray that are insincere
   - [x] Insincere compliments
   - [x] Lies that involve betrayal
   - [ ] Lying to get out of trouble
   - [ ] Cheating the system to get ahead or stay out of trouble
   - [ ] Lying and cheating to make money
   - [ ] Failing to follow through on a promise
   - [ ] Other:______________________

3. Finish this sentence: "I would want someone to be honest when giving me feedback because ..."

I need to know!

today's session

What is God teaching you from this story?

1. What two contrasts are made in Proverbs 11:20?

twisted minds → detestable

blameless conduct → delight

2. Why are lies taken so personally (see Proverbs 12:22)?

faithful vs unfaithful

– can't trust

3. How is it true that stolen food tastes like gravel (Proverbs 20:17)?

guilt makes it sour

4. How can you be a false witness and not be in a courtroom (Proverbs 19:29)?

lie about another person

&

actions

5. How does a truthful witness save lives (Proverbs 14:25)?

truth wins!

→ become a follower of Christ!

7

Learning from the Story

In horseshoe groups of 6-8, explore these questions.

1. In terms of honesty, where are you living right now? Check one.
   - ☐ In the light. This is very important to me.
   - ☐ In a bit of shade. I admit I color the truth to suit myself, though I'm basically honest.
   - ☐ In the half-light. I have benefited from dishonesty, but I've turned my life around.
   - ☐ In the shifting shadows. I'm usually honest, but sometimes I can tell a doozie!
   - ☐ In the dark! I need to quit cheating and lying right now.
   - ☒ Other: Fudge when dealing w/ people!.

2. Finish this sentence: "Dishonesty is a serious sin because ..."

   it offends God who is the truth, and causes great harm to people.

3. What thought inspires you most to be honest? Check one.
   - ☐ Lying is a sin others find hard to forgive.
   - ☐ Cheaters and liars don't get away with it forever.
   - + ☒ God delights in the blameless.
   - – ☐ God detests lying lips.
   - ☐ Other: ______________________.

life change lessons

How can you apply this session to your life?

Write your answers here.

1. What is the root cause of dishonesty?

   Sin nature
   Self-centeredness
   (pride greed)

2. What are steps to taking dishonesty seriously?

   Open eyes to fudging.
   Don't say anything?

Caring Time

15-20 minutes

CARING TIME

Remain in horseshoe groups of 6-8.

This is the time to develop and express your care for each other. Begin by asking group members to answer this question:

"How can we be more honest with one another in this group?"

Pray for these needs as well as the concerns people gave on the Prayer/Praise Report. Include prayer for the empty chair.

If you would like to pray silently, say "Amen" when you have finished your prayer, so that the next person will know when to start.

Reference Notes

BIBLE STUDY NOTES

Use these notes to gain further understanding of the text as you study on your own:

PROVERBS 14:25

witness. A witness has tthe power to either save life or destory it through deceitful testimony.

PROVERBS 19:28

swallows. To practice of evil is a delight to the wicked.

PROVERBS 20:17

gravel. This is an apt picture of the long-term consequences of sin. At first, getting away with something is sweet, but in the end we are left with the remains of our broken character.

notes

Session

8

The Discipline Dilemma

Proverbs 12:1; 13:13,18,24; 15:32; 19:20; 21:11; 27:5-6,17; 28:23; 29:17

Prepare for the Session

	READINGS	REFLECTIVE QUESTIONS
Monday	Proverbs 13:13	Why can it be difficult to listen to instructions and respect commands? Which person is hardest for you to take commands or correction from?
Tuesday	Proverbs 13:18; 19:20	What advice have you ignored to your harm in life? Why did you ignore that advice? What advice or discipline has helped you the most?
Wednesday	Proverbs 12:1; 15:32	Whose advice do you almost always listen to? What characteristics does this person possess that makes you want to listen to and follow him or her? What can you learn from this model?
Thursday	Proverbs 21:11	How are discipline and education related? What are some key lessons you've learned in life as a result of discipline or punishment?
Friday	Proverbs 27:5-6; 28:23	What friends have you had to correct? What was the result? Would you do this again, or was it just too difficult to attempt again? What friends have you been hiding your true feelings from?
Saturday	Proverbs 27:17	Who's a sharpener in your life? Is the sharpening mutual? How does sharpening benefit you?
Sunday	Proverbs 13:24; 29:17	How did discipline help you as a child? Was your childhood a good model? How are you disciplining your children?

OUR GOALS FOR THIS SESSION ARE:

BIBLE STUDY

- To understand the difficulty and reward of receiving correction
- To learn to offer correction and discipline to our friends and children
- To be motivated to learn even from angry and insulting forms of correction

LIFE CHANGE

- To list criticisms you frequently hear, and consider what God may be teaching you
- To spend time with a friend who sharpens you and discuss ways to keep sharpening each other
- To memorize and meditate on Proverbs 12:1

Icebreaker

10-15 minutes

GATHERING THE PEOPLE

Form horseshoe groups of 6-8.

Correction. Depending on time, choose one or two questions, or answer all three. Go around the group on question 1 and let everyone share. Then go around again on questions 2 and/or 3.

1. When you were a child, what form of discipline did your parents most often utilize to train you? Check one and tell briefly how you felt about their apporach.

- [x] Spanking
- [ ] Sit in a corner/Timeouts
- [ ] Couldn't play with friends
- [ ] Couldn't watch television
- [ ] No snacks
- [ ] Other: ______________

Only for severe infractions!

2. Describe a time when you got lost. Where were you trying to go? Why did you get lost? How did you find your way?

Working in W. Va!
- flat area
- no compass
- never been to area

3. When I am forced to tell a peer what he or she ought to do, I ...

- ☐ Pray to be raptured
- ☐ Call to make sure he or she's in a good mood
- ☑ Drive around the block a few times to gain the courage necessary – "put it off"
- ☐ Write down my thoughts so I say the right words the right way
- ☐ I never tell anyone else what he or she ought to do
- ☐ Other: ________________________________

Bible Study

30-45 minutes

The Scripture for this week:

LEARNING FROM THE BIBLE

PROVERBS 12:1; 13:13,18,24; 15:32; 19:20; 21:11; 27:5-6,17; 28:23; 29:17

Whoever loves instruction loves knowledge, but one who hates correction is stupid (Proverbs 12:1).

The one who has contempt for instruction will pay the penalty, but the one who respects a command will be rewarded (Proverbs 13:13).

Poverty and disgrace come to those who ignore instruction, but the one who accepts rebuke will be honored (Proverbs 13:18).

The one who will not use the rod hates his son, but the one who loves him disciplines him diligently (Proverbs 13:24).

Anyone who ignores instruction despises himself, but whoever listens to correction acquires good sense (Proverbs 15:32).

Listen to counsel and receive instruction so that you may be wise in later life (Proverbs 19:20).

When a mocker is punished, the inexperienced become wiser; when one teaches a wise man, he acquires knowledge (Proverbs 21:11).

Better an open reprimand than concealed love. The wounds of a friend are trustworthy, but the kisses of an enemy are excessive (Proverbs 27:5-6).

BIBLE STUDY (cont'd)

Iron sharpens iron, and one man sharpens another (Proverbs 27:17).

One who rebukes a person will later find more favor than one who flatters with his tongue (Proverbs 28:23).

Discipline your son, and he will give you comfort; he will also give you delight (Proverbs 29:17).

...about today's session

A WORD FROM THE LEADER

Write your answers here.

1. What are some examples of people needing correction?

2 year olds - Clayton
boys playing together
adults doing the job the wrong way

2. Why do we resent correction?

Old nature
Don't like to be told what to do.
Hurts our pride.

3. What does authority have to do with correction?

Some one needs to be in charge.
and they must set the standard.
God or boss!

Identifying with the Story

In horseshoe groups of 6-8, explore questions as time allows.

1. Tell a story about someone correcting you in public and embarrassing you.

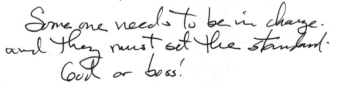

Congregational meetings.

2. Identify each example of correction below as wise or foolish.

W or F ____ Honking and shouting to another driver to slow down and be careful

____ Writing a note to an inattentive waitress explaining why she got a low tip

W ____ Grounding your son for two weeks for borrowing the car without permission

W ____ Explaining to an employee that he eventually will be fired if he cannot smile and speak politely to customers

F ____ Speaking out to a stranger who steps on your foot carelessly

F ____ Telling an angry person to "calm down and get a grip"

!!! W ____ Telling your spouse that spending is getting too high and there is a need to cut back

3. What is your actual attitude toward correction (not necessarily your ideal reaction)? Check the closest response.

- ☐ I've worked hard to get where I am, and I don't need correction.
- ☐ I don't resent correction; I welcome it.
- ☐ I think people could help me better by not correcting me.
- ☐ Correction is only for parents or employers to give.
- ☒ I know I should learn from correction, but I'm too proud to accept it easily.
- ☐ Other: ______________________________.

8

today's session

What is God teaching you from this story?

1. How is it true that a person who hates correction hates himself?

Yes – can never improve! Holding himself back

2. Is correction only for fools? Why or why not?

No - a smart man has many advisors.

TODAY'S SESSION (cont'd)

3. What are some common mistakes in spanking children?

4. How is it true that one who does not spank his child hates him or her?

5. Why should we appreciate correction from a friend?

Learning from the Story

In horseshoe groups of 6-8, explore these questions.

1. How are you right now at receiving correction? Check one.

   ☐ I'd rather visit the dentist.
   ☐ I enjoy it because I like returning the insult.
   ☐ I don't enjoy it, and I often come back with anger or an insult.
   ☐ I can take it from a friend but not from a stranger.
   ☐ I can take it from a stranger but not from a friend.
   ☐ Other: ______________________

2. How would your life be changed if you started learning from your critics?

3. What would help you receive correction more gracefully? Check one.

   ☐ Only brain surgery would help me!
   ☐ If I prayed for and studied God's wisdom on humility.
   ☐ If I learned to separate the anger from the truth of the criticism.
   ☐ If I learned to listen more and think less about what to say in return.
   ☐ Other: ______________________

life change lessons

How can you apply this session to your life?

Write your answers here.

1. How is discipline like pruning?

"Correction to do it right
(Helps us grow!)

2. How would things be different if we welcomed correction?

People would be more inclined to give us correction.
Our attitude would be better!

Caring Time

15-20 minutes

CARING TIME

Remain in horseshoe groups of 6-8.

This is the time to develop and express your care for each other. Begin by asking group members this question:

"How can we sharpen one another in this group?"

8

Pray for a good sharpening relationship in the group as well as for the concerns on the Prayer/Praise Report. Include prayer for the empty chair.

If you would like to pray silently, say "Amen" when you have finished your prayer, so that the next person will know when to start.

Reference Notes

BIBLE STUDY NOTES

Use these notes to gain further understanding of the text as you study on your own:

PROVERBS 13:24

the rod. In this culture the rod was used for spanking. Proverbs consistently reinforces the importance of discipline, regardless of the method of discipline or punishment (10:13; 22:15; 29:15).

PROVERBS 15:32

instruction. God's discipline or moral correction is included in His love for us. Hebrews, as well as other New Testament books, repeats that truth (Heb. 12:7-11). We are to heed discipline or regret foolishness (5:11-12).

PROVERBS 28:23

Rebukes are welcomed by the wise. But flattery is never effective with the wise and discerning.

Session

9

Money ... Nobody Has Enough

Proverbs 11:24-26; 19:17; 22:7; 23:4-5; 27:23-27; 28:8,27

Prepare for the Session

	READINGS	REFLECTIVE QUESTIONS
Monday	Proverbs 11:24-26	Do you hold on to what you have with white knuckles? Why or why not? What are some ways you could be more generous?
Tuesday	Proverbs 19:17	How will God repay kindness? Knowing this, will you be more generous? Where will you start?
Wednesday	Proverbs 22:7	Do you feel enslaved by your debts? How much power do your creditors have over you?
Thursday	Proverbs 23:4-5	Why are riches so hard to obtain? How has pursuit of wealth hurt your life? The life of your family? What is behind an obsession with money?
Friday	Proverbs 27:23-27	How well do you know the condition of your finances? How much interest do you pay every month on credit cards? Think of reasons why God would want you to have your finances organized.
Saturday	Proverbs 28:8	Do you belived God will bring justice for wrongs done in this life? If your brother suddenly needed cash for a major problem and you could help him financially, would you charge him interest?
Sunday	Proverbs 28:27	What is your definition of "poor"? Why do you think it's easy to turn our eyes away from the poor? What does God want you to do?

OUR GOALS FOR THIS SESSION ARE:

BIBLE STUDY

- To understand that saving is better than spending
- To understand that giving is better than wasting
- To be motivated to make a budget, give according to God's plan, and use wisdom in saving

LIFE CHANGE

- To make a budget and review it with a trusted friend
- To take a class on money matters
- To memorize and meditate on Proverbs 11:24

Icebreaker

10-15 minutes

GATHERING THE PEOPLE

Form horseshoe groups of 6-8.

Money Sense. Depending on time, choose one or two questions, or answer all three. Go around the group on question 1 and let everyone share. Then go around again on questions 2 and 3.

1. Finish the following statement: "If I could take back one item in our house and get my money back, it would be ..." Check one.

   - [ ] That ugly lamp
   - [ ] The television
   - [ ] The golf clubs
   - [x] The shoes in that closet
   - [ ] The wedding dress that has been hanging in the closet for years
   - [ ] Other: ______________________

2. Are you a person who is more proud when you buy something expensive or when you get "the deal of a lifetime"? What did you purchase in the last six months that you take the most pride in? Why?

   "deal"
   car – it's over!

3. What was the favorite gift you ever received when you were a teenager? Who gave it to you? Why did it mean so much to you?

Bible Study

30-45 minutes

The Scriptures for this week:

LEARNING FROM THE BIBLE

PROVERBS 11:24-26; 19:17; 22:7; 23:4-5; 27:23-27; 28:8,27

One person gives freely, yet gains more; another withholds what is right, only to become poor. A generous person will be enriched, and the one who gives a drink of water will receive water. People will curse anyone who hoards grain, but a blessing will come to the one who sells it (Proverbs 11:24-26).

Kindness to the poor is a loan to the LORD, and He will give a reward to the lender (Proverbs 19:17).

The rich rule over the poor, and the borrower is a slave to the lender (Proverbs 22:7).

Don't wear yourself out to get rich; stop giving your attention to it. As soon as your eyes fly to it, it disappears, for it makes wings for itself and flies like an eagle to the sky (Proverbs 23:4-5).

Know well the condition of your flock, and pay attention to your herds, for wealth is not forever; not even a crown lasts for all time. When hay is removed and new growth appears and the grain from the hills is gathered in, lambs will provide your clothing, and goats, the price of a field; there will be enough goat's milk for your food—food for your household and nourishment for your servants (Proverbs 27:23-27).

Whoever increases his wealth through excessive interest collects it for one who is kind to the poor (Proverbs 28:8).

The one who gives to the poor will not be in need, but one who turns his eyes away will receive many curses (Proverbs 28:27).

...about today's session

A WORD FROM THE LEADER

Write your answers here.

1. Is money the root of all evil?

2. How is God's view of money balanced between extremes?

3. How will God's philosophy of money benefit you?

Identifying with the Story

In horseshoe groups of 6-8, explore questions as time allows.

1. Tell a story about the most foolish expenditure you ever made.

2. How do you rate on the financial wisdom scale? Check one.

   - ☐ Money disintegrates in my wallet and disappears.
   - ☐ I'm so tight I bring a calculator to make tips to the exact penny.
   - ☒ I'm so tight I still have several pennies from my preschool days.
   - ☐ I did buy the Brooklyn Bridge and swamp land in Alaska.
   - ☐ I spend money so fast that I look like a card dealer at a casino.
   - ☐ I'm pretty good, but I have enough credit cards to play a hand of rummy.
   - ☐ I do fairly well, but I won't be able to retire until I'm 105.
   - ☐ I give money away so fast that the scam artists have me on their most wanted lists.

3. What has been your actual experience with money? Check one.

- [ ] I started off with money and have had it fairly easy.
- [ ] I started off with money, but I've gotten down to just getting by.
- [ ] I started alright, but I've built up debts that make life hard.
- [x] I started with little, but I've managed to save and invest.
- [ ] I got into a huge debt hole, but I've paid it off.
- [ ] Other: ______________________________.

today's session

What is God teaching you from this story?

1. Why is getting rich not worth giving our lives to?

   It soon disappears, → disappointment!
   → no value in the end

2. Why do generous people usually have plenty?

   Because God blesses the generous person!

3. What is the key difference between a hoarder and a giver?

   hoarders — for himself
   givers — for others

4. Does the Bible forbid borrowing money? Why or why not?

   No! but discourages it.
   "slave to the lender"

5. What steps should you take to know the condition of your finances?

   Know expense
   " income
   Have a plan (budget)
   Future?

9

Learning from the Story

In horseshoe groups of 6-8, explore these questions.

1. What important steps are you taking right now to be financially wise? Check all that apply.

   - [ ] I'm saving to have extra for emergencies.
   - [ ] I'm paying back my debts with a plan to be debt-free.
   - [x] I've made a budget, and I'm finding ways to stick to it and not spend more.
   - [x] I'm downsizing so I can live on less, save more, give more.
   - [ ] I'm investing for retirement, and I've gotten good advice about how much to invest and how to invest it.
   - [ ] Other: ______________________________.

2. How would your life be changed if you were debt-free and had savings and investments?

   It is debt free!

3. How is your financial situation? Check one.

   - [ ] I feel like I'm in a hole and can't get out.
   - [x] I need to be careful, but I have savings and don't have unsecured debt.
   - [ ] I'm not doing great, and I need advice about budgets, saving, and investing.
   - [ ] I'm on a plan to get where I need to be, but it will take some time.
   - [ ] Other: ______________________________.

life change lessons

How can you apply this session to your life?

Write your answers here.

1. What tends to be left out of budgets?

   – Emergency funds
   – Maintenance funds

2. What makes an investment strategy wise?

   Can't lose it's value.

Caring Time

15-20 minutes

CARING TIME

Remain in horseshoe groups of 6-8.

This is the time to develop and express your care for each other. Begin by asking group members to answer this question:

"How can we pray for your finances?"

Pray for a good sharpening relationship in the group as well as for the concerns on the Prayer/Praise Report. Include prayer for the empty chair.

If you would like to pray silently, say "Amen" when you have finished your prayer, so that the next person will know when to start.

Reference Notes

BIBLE STUDY NOTES

Use these notes to gain further understanding of the text as you study on your own:

PROVERBS 11:24 ***gives freely, yet gains.*** This is a paradox. Generosity, not hoarding, is the path to prosperity.

PROVERBS 22:7 ***slave.*** Often in ancient culture people had to enslave themselves to pay off debts. The slave here refers to anyone in debt.

PROVERBS 27:23-27 This passage celebrates the security and the cycle of an agricultural society.

9

notes

Session

10

Doubtful Trust in God

Proverbs 10:29; 15:11,29; 16:5,9,33; 18:10; 19:21,23; 20:24,27; 29:25

Prepare for the Session

	READINGS	REFLECTIVE QUESTIONS
Monday	Proverbs 10:29; 18:10	What experiences lead you to believe or not believe that knowing God is a "stronghold" for you?
Tuesday	Proverbs 15:11; 20:27	How real is your sense that God knows your thoughts and emotions? Is this a comfort or a concern for you, and why?
Wednesday	Proverbs 16:9; 20:24	What evidence do you see that God has been planning the steps of your life? Are there ways life could have been easier if you'd followed His way?
Thursday	Proverbs 16:33; 19:21	In your life, what unexpected directions have you experienced as a result of God's leadership and love?
Friday	Proverbs 15:29; 16:5	Do you believe in God's justice? Do you believe that your actions affect your prayer life?
Saturday	Proverbs 19:23	In what ways does God ultimately protect you from evil?
Sunday	Proverbs 29:25	Are you a people-pleaser more than a God-pleaser? Why is it that we sometimes want to please other people more than we want to please God?

OUR GOALS FOR THIS SESSION ARE:

BIBLE STUDY

- To believe in God's total knowledge of and influence over His creation
- To believe in God's justice and love for those who follow Him
- To be motivated to seek a relationship with God in keeping with wisdom

LIFE CHANGE

- To make a list of truths known only by special revelation of God
- To write an explanation of reasons to have faith in God
- To memorize and meditate on Proverbs 18:10

Icebreaker

10-15 minutes

GATHERING THE PEOPLE

Form horseshoe groups of 6-8.

Trust Factors. Depending on time, choose one or two questions, or answer all three. Go around the group on question 1 and let everyone share. Then go around again on questions 2 and/or 3.

1. Finish the following statement: "When I was a teenager, the person who believed in me most was ..." Check one.

   ☒ My mom ☐ My dad
   ☐ My best friend ☐ My girlfriend or boyfriend
   ☐ My boss ☐ Other: ________________

2. How did this person prove he or she had faith in you and your abilities?

3. How would you describe the way you feel about your dad in this era of your life? Check one.

   ☑ ~~Best~~ friend ☐ Confidant
   ☐ Mentor ☐ Enemy
   ☐ Purposefully disconnected ☐ Other: ________________

Bible Study

30-45 minutes

LEARNING FROM THE BIBLE

PROVERBS 10:29; 15:11,29; 16:5,9,33; 18:10; 19:21,23; 20:24,27; 29:25

The Scripture for this week:

The way of the LORD is a stronghold for the honorable, but destruction awaits the malicious (Proverbs 10:29).

Sheol and Abaddon lie open before the LORD—how much more, human hearts (Proverbs 15:11).

The LORD is far from the wicked, but He hears the prayer of the righteous (Proverbs 15:29).

Everyone with a proud heart is detestable to the LORD; be assured, he will not go unpunished (Proverbs 16:5).

A man's heart plans his way, but the LORD determines his steps (Proverbs 16:9).

The lot is cast into the lap, but its every decision is from the LORD (Proverbs 16:33).

The name of the LORD is a strong tower; the righteous run to it and are protected (Proverbs 18:10).

Many plans are in a man's heart, but the LORD'S decree will prevail (Proverbs 19:21).

The fear of the LORD leads to life; one will sleep at night without danger (Proverbs 19:23).

A man's steps are determined by the LORD, so how can anyone understand his own way (Proverbs 20:24)?

A person's breath is the lamp of the LORD, searching the innermost parts (Proverbs 20:27).

The fear of man is a snare, but the one who trusts in the LORD is protected (Proverbs 29:25).

...about today's session

A WORD FROM THE LEADER

Write your answers here.

1. How is wisdom the creation of God?

   He is the Creator & ∴ knows everything!

2. How does unbelief lead to misunderstanding in life?

   Unbelief leads to not knowing the right way!

3. How is the world's wisdom lacking in truth and value?

   "Worldly" - by sight
   Doesn't know beginning & end!

Identifying with the Story

In horseshoe groups of 6-8, explore questions as time allows.

1. Tell a story about how you learned God is in charge of your life.

   Call to Korea

2. How big a part does God play in your daily life? Check one.

   - [ ] God is not in my thoughts much when I am working, driving, or busy.
   - [x] God is mostly in the quiet moments in have every day and when I am in a worship service or small group.
   - [ ] I know God is there, but I have little sense of Him most of the time.
   - [x] Sometimes I sense God throughout the day, and other times I tend to forget Him.
   - [ ] God is always there, though I sometimes choose to ignore Him.
   - [ ] Other: ____.

3. What part does wisdom play in your daily life? Check one.

- [x] I would like to act with more wisdom, ~~but I usually fly by the seat of my pants.~~
- [ ] Sometimes I think before I act, but I don't know much about Proverbs and wisdom.
- [ ] I'm memorizing some verses from Proverbs and trying to make them part of my life.
- [ ] I've been doing things my way for so long I'm afraid it will be hard to learn new ways.
- [ ] Other: ______________________.

today's session

What is God teaching you from this story?

1. What are Sheol and Abaddon?

Death & hell.

2. Why can't we predict how things will turn out?

Don't know the beginning & the end.

3. Why do people doubt God's justice?

See injustice in the world. It's God's fault!!

4. Does our obedience or disobedience have any effect on how God answers prayer?

Yes! Prayers hindered by disobedience. Won't answer! Reward — answered prayer!

10

5. How did a tower provide protection in ancient societies?

"fortress"

Learning from the Story

In horseshoe groups of 6-8, explore these questions.

1. What needs to happen to increase your trust in God's justice and favor?

2. How is your trust in God when life is hard? Check one.
   - ☐ I know God is in control, but my mind fixes on the circumstances.
   - ☐ I want to know God is in control, but I have doubts.
   - ☐ I only tend to think about God after the initial shock wears off.
   - ☐ I only tend to think about God after the danger is over.
   - ☐ Faith in God is the only thing that gets me through hard times.
   - ☐ Other: ______________________________.

3. In what ways are we people-pleasers instead of God-pleasers?

life change lessons

How can you apply this session to your life?

Write your answers here.

1. What kinds of experiences make people doubt God's knowledge, goodness, or justice?

2. How does the universe argue for the reality of God?

Caring Time

15-20 minutes

CARING TIME

Remain in horseshoe groups of 6-8.

This is the time to develop and express your care for each other. Begin by asking group members to answer this question:

"How can we pray for your faith?"

Pray for the faith of the group to grow as well as for the concerns on the Prayer/Praise Report. Include prayer for the empty chair.

If you would like to pray silently, say "Amen" when you have finished your prayer, so that the next person will know when to start.

BIBLE STUDY NOTES

Reference Notes

Use these notes to gain further understanding of the text as you study on your own:

PROVERBS 15:11

Sheol and Abaddon. This is probably an allusion to the fact that God sees the dead in their graves or in their eternal homes. How much more should God be able to see the hearts of living people?

PROVERBS 16:9

plans his way. God's sovereignty over our lives should not discourage us from planning and setting goals. However, we need God's wisdom to guide us.

PROVERBS 20:27

searching the innermost parts. King David asked God to search him out (Ps. 139:23). (See also Hebrews 4:12 for another way of being "found" by God.)

10

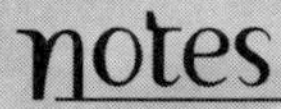

Session

11

Living Life on Purpose

Proverbs 10:4-5; 12:24,27; 13:4; 14:4,23; 20:1; 23:20-21; 24:27

Prepare for the Session

	READINGS	REFLECTIVE QUESTIONS
Monday	Proverbs 10:4; 12:24	What areas of your life inspire you to hard work? What are the rewards of hard work?
Tuesday	Proverbs 13:4; 14:23	Do you know people who work hard for what they have? Do you know people who are wasting their talents? How are you spending your life?
Wednesday	Proverbs 10:5	How much is procrastination a problem for you? Do you think most people procrastinate a great deal, or are most people goal-oriented achievers?
Thursday	Proverbs 14:4	Do you ever think it would be easier not even to try? Would you rather work hard and have some of the things you want or relax more and do without?
Friday	Proverbs 24:27	Do you have trouble prioritizing on big tasks? Do you leap in without a plan? Why do you think setting priorities is important in the Christian life?
Saturday	Proverbs 12:27	Do you take good care of the things you have? Which of your possessions is most important to you? Why?
Sunday	Proverbs 20:1; 23:20-21	How much is self-control a problem for you (alcohol, food, sexuality)? Which of your friends is most self-controlled? Which has the least self-control? Which of these two friends is happier and more successful in your eyes?

OUR GOALS FOR THIS SESSION ARE:

BIBLE STUDY
- To believe in the wisdom of diligence and self-control
- To understand principles of work and addiction
- To be motivated to plan and implement a life lived purposefully

LIFE CHANGE
- To chart the areas of your life and consider balancing time and energy
- To focus on a neglected area of life for a week and pray for future motivation
- To memorize and meditate on Proverbs 13:4

Icebreaker

10-15 minutes

GATHERING THE PEOPLE

Form horseshoe groups of 6-8.

Working Hard or Hardly Working? Depending on time, choose one or two questions, or answer all three. Go around the group on question 1 and let everyone share. Then go around again on questions 2 and/or 3.

1. Finish this statement: "When it came to doing chores when I was a kid ..." Check one.

   ☐ I waited until the very last minute to get the job done.
   ☐ I normally did a poor job the first time and was forced to redo the job a second time so the work was done to my parent's standards.
   ☐ I found a way to get my brothers and sisters to do my chores.
   ☐ I realized that if I waited long enough, mom or dad would do them for me, so I waited.
   ☐ I didn't have to do chores.
   ☑ Other: Don't remember.

2. If you could be anyone in the world, who would it be? Describe what a normal workday would probably like for this person.

   Billy Graham

3. If the person who spends the most time with you picked one of the following words to describe the way you live your life, he or she would most likely choose ... Check one.

- ☐ TV-aholic
- ☒ Workaholic
- ☐ Friend-aholic
- ☐ Sports-aholic
- ☐ Web-aholic
- ☐ Other:____________________

Bible Study

30-45 minutes

The Scripture for this week:

LEARNING FROM THE BIBLE

PROVERBS 10:4-5; 12:24,27; 13:4; 14:4,23; 20:1; 23:20-21; 24:27

Idle hands make one poor, but diligent hands bring riches (Proverbs 10:4).

The son who gathers during summer is prudent; the son who sleeps during harvest is disgraceful (Proverbs 10:5).

The diligent hand will rule, but laziness will lead to forced labor (Proverbs 12:24).

A lazy man doesn't roast his game, but to a diligent man, his wealth is precious (Proverbs 12:27).

The slacker craves, yet has nothing, but the diligent is fully satisfied (Proverbs 13:4).

Where there are no oxen, the feeding-trough is empty, but an abundant harvest comes through the strength of an ox (Prov. 14:4).

There is profit in all hard work, but endless talk leads only to poverty (Proverbs 14:23).

Wine is a mocker, beer is a brawler, and whoever staggers because of them is not wise (Proverbs 20:1).

Don't associate with those who drink too much wine, or with those who gorge themselves on meat. For the drunkard and the glutton will become poor, and grogginess will clothe them in rags (Proverbs 23:20-21).

Complete your outdoor work, and prepare your field; afterwards, build your house (Proverbs 24:27).

...about today's session

A WORD FROM THE LEADER

Write your answers here.

1. Is work part of God's curse on this world? Explain.

Yes and know.
- Originally created to work.
- Sin added difficulties to it. – sweat – thorns

2. How did work figure into God's plan for humanity?

Adam & Eve tended the garden.
- made to rule over the earth.

Identifying with the Story

In horseshoe groups of 6-8, explore questions as time allows.

1. What is the hardest job you've ever done?

Company Commander in Korea

2. How do you honestly feel about work? Check one.

- [ ] A robot could do what I do, and I don't enjoy it.
- [ ] I haven't found my life's work yet, but I enjoy earning a living.
- [ ] I'd rather have a hammock in the backyard or take up golf or fishing.
- [ ] I'd rather watch cooking shows all day than do all that work myself.
- [ ] I'd like to get paid for the work I do at home.
- [x] Work isn't always fun, but I enjoy what I am doing and feel skilled at it.
- [ ] Other: ______________________________.

3. How motivated are you in your work? Check one.

   - [ ] I'm more addicted to video games and entertainment than work.
   - [ ] I hit the snooze button four or five times before dragging myself out of bed to get ready for work.
   - [ ] After a few cups of coffee, I'm ready to hit it hard.
   - [ ] I don't mind, but I wish others would do a little more of their share.
   - [ ] I want the corner office before I'm too old to enjoy it.
   - [x] I'm satisfied and enjoy getting better at what I do.
   - [ ] Other: ________________________________.

today's session

What is God teaching you from this story?

1. What is the relationship between hard work and success?

   Go together. Can't have one w/o the other.

2. What does it mean to gather in the summer?

   Work for a harvest

3. What does Proverbs 14:4 mean about oxen and a harvest?

   Takes hard work (strength) to get a harvest

4. What does Proverbs 24:27 mean about first preparing the ground and then building the house?

   You need food to live on first, then comfort.

5. How is addiction a mocker?

   – make a fool out of you!

11

Learning from the Story

In horseshoe groups of 6-8, explore these questions.

1. What areas of your life need more diligence?

2. What are your work habits like? Check one.

   ☒ I get up early, get it done, and get home to rest.
   ☐ I get a late start and finish late.
   ☐ I waste time during the day, but I get it done.
   ☐ I do get distracted at times, but I finish my work and stay ahead.
   ☐ I really need to focus so I can do more and waste less time.
   ☐ Other: ____________________________

3. What can help someone who is addicted, whether it be to a substance or a behavior?

life change lessons

How can you apply this session to your life?

Write your answers here.

1. How do you balance relationships, pleasure, and work?

2. How does the universe argue for the reality of God?

Caring Time

15-20 minutes

CARING TIME

Remain in horseshoe groups of 6-8.

This is the time to develop and express your care for each other. Begin by asking group members to answer this question:

"How can we pray for you to have more balance in your life?"

Pray for balance in the group as well as for the concerns on the Prayer/Praise Report. Include prayer for the empty chair.

If you would like to pray silently, say "Amen" when you have finished your prayer, so that the next person will know when to start.

Reference Notes

BIBLE STUDY NOTES

Use these notes to gain further understanding of the text as you study on your own:

PROVERBS 10:4

poor. In Proverbs poverty is usually associated with laziness or a lack of discipline.

PROVERBS 10:5

harvest. Solomon's culture was agricultural. He often uses the image of harvest to illustrate a person who understands the discipline of taking care of himself. In chapter 6 he used the hard-working ant to make the same comparison (6:6-8).

PROVERBS 12:27

roast. This may refer to the preparation of food or to preparation for the hunt. The point is that the lazy person doesn't adequately provide for himself and his family.

PROVERBS 20:1

Wine ... beer. Wine here refers to fermented grape juice. Beer was made from barley, dates, or pomegranates. Priests were forbidden to drink beer because it was so intoxicating.

PROVERBS 24:27

afterwards, build your house. Since the culture was agrarian, the first priority was establishing the land and planting the seed. After that the people could build houses and establish families.

notes

Session

12

Our Feeling Frenzy

Proverbs 14:10,13,30; 15:13,30; 18:14; 25:20

Prepare for the Session

	READINGS	REFLECTIVE QUESTIONS
Monday	Proverbs 14:10	How emotional are you? What is positive about being emotional? What is negative about it?
Tuesday	Proverbs 14:13	Do you find yourself faking happiness around other people? What sadness might others around you be hiding?
Wednesday	Proverbs 14:30	How do stress and conflict affect your health and your state of mind?
Thursday	Proverbs 15:13	Why does sadness seem to break your spirit? How can others help you heal?
Friday	Proverbs 15:30	Who encourages you with cheerfulness? How powerful is a good laugh with a friend or loved one?
Saturday	Proverbs 18:14	Would you prefer a week of the flu or a week of depression? Why?
Sunday	Proverbs 25:20	What do people with a heavy heart need? Who do you know that needs you to come alongside him or her?

OUR GOALS FOR THIS SESSION ARE:

BIBLE STUDY

- To understand how emotion can be more powerful than intellect
- To understand joy as a foretaste of life with God
- To understand how to help people who are depressed or sad

LIFE CHANGE

- To keep a journal of emotions for a day or week to notice trends
- To list people in your life and pray for some who seem depressed
- To memorize and meditate on Proverbs 14:10

Icebreaker

10-15 minutes

GATHERING THE PEOPLE

Form horseshoe groups of 6-8.

Big Boys Don't Cry. Depending on time, choose one or two questions, or answer all three. Go around the group on question 1 and let everyone share. Then go around again on questions 2 and/or 3.

1. What is the craziest thing you ever did because you were "caught up in the moment"?

   Took Greek - 6 week summer course

2. Which of the following emotions best describes the way you're feeling right now? Check one.

   - [ ] Elation
   - [ ] Contentment
   - [x] Depression
   - [ ] Other: "Bittersweet"
   - [x] Excitement
   - [ ] Apathy
   - [ ] Hopelessness

3. Considering your answer to number 2, why do you think you are feeling that particular emotion today? Check one.

   - [ ] Didn't get my coffee
   - [ ] No particular reason
   - [ ] For the most part, I always feel this way
   - [ ] Other: ____________
   - [ ] A situation at work
   - [x] A situation at home, Moving!

Bible Study

30-45 minutes

The Scripture for this week:

LEARNING FROM THE BIBLE

PROVERBS 14:10,13,30; 15:13,30; 18:14; 25:20

The heart knows its own bitterness, and no outsider shares in its joy (Proverbs 14:10).

Even in laughter a heart may be sad, and joy may end in grief (Proverbs 14:13).

A tranquil heart is life to the body, but jealousy is rottenness to the bones (Proverbs 14:30).

A joyful heart makes a face cheerful, but a sad heart produces a broken spirit (Proverbs 15:13).

Bright eyes cheer the heart; good news strengthens the bones (Proverbs 15:30).

A man's spirit can endure sickness, but who can survive a broken spirit? (Proverbs 18:14).

Singing songs to a troubled heart is like taking off clothing on a cold day, or like pouring vinegar on soda (Proverbs 25:20).

...about today's session

A WORD FROM THE LEADER

Write your answers here.

1. How do different emotions affect us?

   Outlook
   Perspective
   Attitude
   Cloud the truth

2. Why are other people's emotions hard to see and understand?

   Try to hide them.
   I Don't get it.

3. What did David write about emotions?

   Songs (Psalms)

12

Identifying with the Story

In horseshoe groups of 6-8, explore questions as time allows.

1. Is it easier for life to bring you joy or depression? Why?

Joy now – but not always so! Who do you trust?

2. When you are depressed, which of these feelings do you experience? Check all that apply.

- [ ] I'm afraid to be around other people.
- [ ] I'm afraid to be alone.
- [ ] I'm afraid of neither being alone nor being with other people.
- [x] I hide it so no one else can see.
- [ ] I find it impossible to hide.
- [ ] I sometimes can't think of a reason for the depression.
- [ ] I generally have a reason, and I know why I am depressed.
- [ ] Other: ______________________.

3. When you are joyful, which of these do you experience? Check all that apply.

- [ ] I try hard not to smile and laugh all day; instead, I try to be serious.
- [ ] I can't hide my joy. I laugh, and my cheeks get tired of grinning.
- [ ] I find an irresistible urge to be around other people and share the joy.
- [x] I find myself hoping that nothing will make the joy end.
- [ ] I become irresponsible and distracted from work and things I need to do.
- [ ] Other: ______________________.

today's session

What is God teaching you from this story?

1. How is an understanding of emotion related to wisdom?

Our relationships to God & others is affected by how we feel!

2. Why is it a mistake to underrate emotion?

We don't realize how much it affects us!
"so powerful"

3. What are two requirements for encouragement?

sincerety & honesty
communication

4. Why do people hide emotions?

- Afraid of what others will think!
- Taught to - esp. males

5. What is the difference between mere happiness and true joy?

Happiness based on circumstances!
- "external"
True Joy = internal - regardless of circumstances

Learning from the Story

In horseshoe groups of 6-8, explore these questions.

1. How much is your life pulled along by emotion?

?- more rational than emotional

2. How do you react when you're depressed? Check all that apply.

- [x] I think about it when I am alone, but I hide it in public.
- [ ] I don't sleep well, and my time alone is the worst.
- [ ] I don't hide it well, and my time in public is the worst.
- [x] I eat more and get less done.
- [ ] I cry a lot and try to stay out of sight.
- [ ] I'm grumpy and easily angered.
- [ ] Other: ______________________

12

LEARNING FROM THE STORY (cont'd)

3. What can you do to help someone who is depressed?

Be there for them.
Encourage them.
Pray w/ & for them!

life change lessons

How can you apply this session to your life?

Write your answers here.

1. Emotional strength can be found in two important actions. What are they?

God's word

Prayer

2. What is one often-overlooked source of encouragement and help?

Promises of God. (Holy Spirit

Caring Time

15-20 minutes

CARING TIME

Remain in horseshoe groups of 6-8.

This is the time to develop and express your care for each other. Begin by asking group members to answer this question:

"How can we pray for your emotional life?"

Pray for the emotional lives of the group members as well as for the concerns on the Prayer/Praise Report. Include prayer for the empty chair.

If you would like to pray silently, say "Amen" when you have finished your prayer, so that the next person will know when to start.

BIBLE STUDY NOTES

Reference Notes

Use these notes to gain further understanding
of the text as you study on your own:

PROVERBS 14:33

laughter. Laughter is good medicine for our souls. However, while it may relieve stress of a person who is suffering, it is only a temporary escape from the reality of struggles.

PROVERBS 15:13

sad heart. Maintaining sadness in our hearts crushes our spirits, creating discouragemen, disillusion, and hopelessness.

PROVERBS 15:30

Bright eyes. This is the sparkle or gleam in the eyes when good news comes. ***strengthens the bones.*** This joy invigorates our body, mind, and spirt.

notes

Session

13

The Fountain of Life

Proverbs 10:19; 11:12; 13:14; 18:2,6,15; 19:8; 21:16; 24:3-4; 27:12; 29:11; 29:20

Prepare for the Session

	READINGS	REFLECTIVE QUESTIONS
Monday	Proverbs 18:2	Why is listening in order to understand wiser than speaking in order to be heard?
Tuesday	Proverbs 18:6	How are you growing in wisdom? Who was the last person you injured by what you said? How do you feel about that in light of this study?
Wednesday	Proverbs 13:14; 19:8	How has wisdom kept you out of trouble? How has folly gotten you into trouble?
Thursday	Proverbs 21:16 27:12	How is a lack of wisdom related to death? Do you know someone who knows he is on a very wrong path, yet he refuses to change? As a friend, what more can you do?
Friday	Proverbs 10:19 29:11,20	How long has it been since your words got you into trouble? Why is it sometimes not enough to say, "I'm sorry"?
Saturday	Proverbs 11:12; 18:6	Have you belittled anyone recently either to his face or behind his back? How does that make you the smaller person?
Sunday	Proverbs 24:3-4	Can your life be described as a well-built house? As a result of this study, what are you going to do to continue to build your life on a foundation of wisdom?

OUR GOALS FOR THIS SESSION ARE:

BIBLE STUDY
- To understand how necessary wisdom is to daily life
- To understand the consequences of folly
- To be motivated to pursue wisdom actively

LIFE CHANGE
- To list the proverbs and principles that have helped you during this series
- To choose one person you need to listen to more and focus on him or her this week
- To memorize and meditate on Proverbs 18:15

Icebreaker

10-15 minutes

GATHERING THE PEOPLE

Form horseshoe groups of 6-8.

Uncommon Sense. Depending on time, choose one or two questions, or answer all three. Go around the group on question 1 and let everyone share. Then go around again on questions 2 and/or 3.

1. Which of the following statements best describes a hoax you got caught up in? Check one.

   ☐ Forward this e-mail to all of your friends and you'll receive a gift or a check for $1,000.00
   ☐ Snipe hunting – looking for an animal that doesn't exist
   ☐ A purchase you made on eBay that never arrived
   ☐ A used car that was a lemon
   ☐ Other: ______________________________

2. Describe the most foolish thing you ever did when you were a teenager. Driving home when too tired! – wrecked

3. Life is a series of decisions. What is the wisest decision you made this week?

Bible Study

30-45 minutes

The Scripture for this week:

LEARNING FROM THE BIBLE

PROVERBS 10:19; 11:12; 13:14; 18:2,6,15; 19:8; 21:16; 24:3-4; 27:12; 29:11; 29:20

When there are many words, sin is unavoidable, but the one who controls his lips is wise (Proverbs 10:19).

Whoever shows contempt for his neighbor lacks sense, but a man with understanding keeps silent (Proverbs 11:12).

A wise man's instruction is a fountain of life, turning people away from the snares of death (Proverbs 13:14).

A fool does not delight in understanding, but only wants to show off his opinions (Proverbs 18:2).

A fool's lips lead to strife, and his mouth provokes a beating (Proverbs 18:6).

The mind of the discerning acquires knowledge, and the ear of the wise seeks it (Proverbs 18:15).

The one who acquires good sense loves himself; one who safeguards understanding finds success (Proverbs 19:8).

The man who strays from the way of wisdom will come to rest in the assembly of the departed spirits (Proverbs 21:16).

A house is built by wisdom, and it is established by understanding; by knowledge the rooms are filled with every precious and beautiful treasure (Proverbs 24:3-4).

The sensible see danger and take cover; the foolish keep going and are punished (Proverbs 27:12).

A fool gives full vent to his anger, but a wise man holds it in check (Proverbs 29:11).

Do you see a man who speaks too soon? There is more hope for a fool than for him (Proverbs 29:20).

...about today's session

A WORD FROM THE LEADER

Write your answers here.

1. How can wisdom seem deceptively easy?

   Much is common sense – "Keeps mouth shut, don't get into trouble"
   (By giving a simple answer too quickly)

2. What does it take to get wisdom not only in your head but also into your actions?

   DESIRE!
   Understanding – by doing what you say.
   (Just do it.)

3. What are common consequences of living foolishly?

   Broken relationships
   Regret
   Bankruptcy
   Guilt
   Sin
   Anger
   Illness
   Emotional pain
   Disappointment

Identifying with the Story

In horseshoe groups of 6-8, explore questions as time allows.

1. What foolish action have you seen someone do recently in public?

   Texting while driving!

2. What is the hardest part about being wise right now? Check one.

   ☐ I've been making mistakes for so long, it's hard to change.
   ☐ I have trouble finding time to memorize proverbs and study wisdom.
   ☒ I forget wisdom in the rush of things.
   ☐ My emotions seem to guide me more than my head.
   ☐ During the heat of the moment, I forget about consequences and the future.
   ☐ Other: ______________________________.

3. If you could gain wisdom in just one area of your life, what would that area be?

today's session

What is God teaching you from this story?

1. How is wisdom a "fountain of life"?

2. How can foolishness be so devastating?

3. In addition to reading from Proverbs, what is another godly source of wisdom, according to Solomon?

4. If listening is crucial to having wisdom, how do the words you speak reflect that wisdom gained or ignored?

5. The greatest wisdom of all can be found in the words of Jesus. Do any of these verses we've studied today remind you of words from the wise heart of Jesus?

Learning from the Story

In horseshoe groups of 6-8, explore these questions.

1. How big of a difference can wisdom make in your life?

BIG!

2. What are your listening habits? Check all that apply.

- [ ] I multi-task, so I usually try to do something else while I'm listening.
- [x] I try to listen to people, but I find myself thinking of replies before they are finished.
- [ ] I can listen to instructions, but I have trouble listening to people express emotions.
- [ ] I listen when I know I need to, but I tune out most small talk.
- [x] I look people in the eye and try to hear every word they say.
- [ ] Other: ____.

3. In your life, what areas of wisdom have you seen improvement in during these 13 studies?

Listening!

life change lessons

How can you apply this session to your life?

Write your answers here.

1. How can listening to and watching the lives of others help you in your quest for wisdom?

Example! – "watch & learn"

2. Although this study is over, how can you continue to learn from the wisdom God placed in the heart of Solomon?

Keep reviewing & studying!

Caring Time

15-20 minutes

CARING TIME

Remain in horseshoe groups of 6-8.

Pray for the concerns on the Prayer/Praise Report, then continue with the evaluation and covenant.

1. Take some time to evaluate the life of your group by using the statements below. Read the first sentence out loud and ask everyone to explain where they would put a dot between the two extremes. When you are finished, go back and give your group an overall grade in the categories of Group Building, Bible Study, and Mission.

GROUP BUILDING

On celebrating life and having fun together, we were more like a ...

wet blanket · **hot tub**

On becoming a caring community, we were more like a ...

prickly porcupine · **cuddly teddy bear**

BIBLE STUDY

On sharing our spiritual stories, we were more like a ...

shallow pond · **spring-fed lake**

On digging into Scripture, we were more like a ...

slow-moving snail · **voracious anteater**

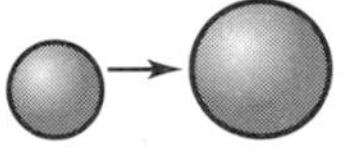

MISSION

On inviting new people into our group, we were more like a ...

barbed-wire fence · **wide-open door**

On stretching our vision for mission, we were more like an ...

ostrich · **eagle**

13

CARING TIME (cont'd)

2. What are some specific areas in which you have grown in this course?

   - ☐ Understanding that fearing God is the foundational life-skill
   - ☐ Motivation to use wise words to heal and encourage others
   - ☐ Focusing on others and making a habit of humility
   - ☐ Developing faith in God's blessing for living honestly
   - ☐ Valuing correction and discipline for myself and others
   - ☐ Truly believing in God's total knowledge and influence over my life and the world around me
   - ☐ Grasping the power of emotions and their value in my life
   - ☐ Other: ______________________________

A covenant is a promise made to another in the presence of God. Its purpose is to indicate your intention to make yourselves available to one another for the fulfillment of the purposes you share in common. If your group is going to continue, in a spirit of prayer work your way through the following sentences, trying to reach an agreement on each statement pertaining to your ongoing life together. Write out your covenant like a contract, stating your purpose, goals, and the ground rules for your group.

1. The purpose of our group will be:

2. Our goals will be:

3. We will meet on ____________________ (day of week).

4. We will meet for _____weeks, after which we will decide if we wish to continue as a group.

5. We will meet from ________ to ________ and we will strive to start on time and end on time.

6. We will meet at ________________________ (place) or we will rotate from house to house.

7. We will agree to the following ground rules for our group (check):

   - ☐ **PRIORITY:** While you are in this course of study, you give the group meetings priority.
   - ☐ **PARTICIPATION:** Everyone is encouraged to participate and no one dominates.
   - ☐ **RESPECT:** Everyone has the right to his or her own opinion, and all questions are encouraged and respected.
   - ☐ **CONFIDENTIALITY:** Anything said in the meeting is never repeated outside the meeting.
   - ☐ **LIFE CHANGE:** We will regularly assess our own life change goals and encourage one another in our pursuit of becoming like Jesus Christ.
   - ☐ **EMPTY CHAIR:** The group stays open to reaching new people at every meeting.
   - ☐ **CARE and SUPPORT:** Permission is given to call upon each other at any time especially in times of crisis. The group will provide care for every member.
   - ☐ **ACCOUNTABILITY:** We agree to let the members of the group hold us accountable to the commitments which each of us make in whatever loving ways we decide upon.
   - ☐ **MISSION:** We will do everything in our power to start a new group.
   - ☐ **MINISTRY:** The group will encourage one another to volunteer and serve in a ministry, and to support missions by giving financially and/or personally serving.

Reference Notes

BIBLE STUDY NOTES

Use these notes to gain further understanding of the text as you study on your own:

PROVERBS 11:12

shows contempt. This refers to despising or belittling.

PROVERBS 13:14

instruction. This is any kind of teaching or training. ***fountain of life***. This refers to the source of spiritual vitality and true fufilment.

PROVERBS 24:3-4

house. Any house, whether individual or family, is grounded in wisdom, strenghten by understanding, and prospered by knowledge.

Acknowledgments:

We sincerely appreciate the great team of people that worked to develop this study on *Proverbs: Uncommon Sense*. Special thanks are extended to Derek Leman for writing this study. We also appreciate the editorial and production team that consisted of Ben Colter, Scott Lee of Scott Lee Designs, Richard Ryan, Lori Mayes. Rick Howerton, Sarah Hogg. and the design team at Powell Creative.

notes

notes

notes

notes

notes

notes

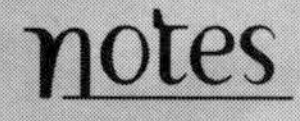

notes

notes

notes

Group Directory

PASS THIS DIRECTORY AROUND AND HAVE YOUR GROUP MEMBERS FILL IN THEIR NAMES AND PHONE NUMBERS.

NAME	PHONE
Castors	
Thing for chair	
Light bulb	